I AM

Reaching Out

MY SISTER'S

to Wounded Women

KEEPER

DENISE GEORGE

CHRISTIAN
FOCUS

I AM

Reaching Out

MY SISTER'S

to Wounded Women

KEEPER

This book encourages Christian women to extend God's love to women who are suffering deep sadness and grief from circumstances such as broken marriages, guilt, loss and abuse. Denise George sensitively shows us how the gospel of our Jesus can meet their greatest needs, as she looks at Jesus' encounters with women in the Gospels and personal stories of contemporary women.

I found *I Am My Sister's Keeper* a genuinely Christian response to particular issues that cause much suffering among many women in today's world. It motivated me to care more deeply for women I meet by sensitively listening to their stories, praying for and with them, showing practical love, and especially by sharing God's love for them in Jesus.

The helpful discussion questions for each chapter make this book valuable for group study where the implications for each of us and for our churches can be explored.

Moya A. Woodhouse
Faculty wife at Moore College
Sydney, Australia

Denise George writes from many years of experience of ministering to women. This book is faithful in portraying the reality of intense suffering in a fallen world, but equally faithful in presenting the resources for healing available to all in Christ. It will be a great resource for Christian women who are concerned to show Christ-like love to those who are suffering.

Sharon James
Conference speaker and author
Leamington Spa, England

CONTENTS

For my son, Dr Christian Timothy George and his incredible wife, Rebecca Pounds George, with eternal love, gratitude and admiration.

Some of the women's names in this book have been changed to protect their privacy.

ACKNOWLEDGEMENTS

With my sincere gratitude to all the women who have allowed me into their lives and into their hearts, and who have shared with me their pain and their personal stories for this book. Thank you, also, to all the wonderful people at Christian Focus Publications: William and Carine MacKenzie, Catherine MacKenzie, Willie and Kate MacKenzie. A hearty thank you to my family, and to my friends, who encourage me, support me, and most important of all, who pray for me as I study, interview, and write.

Love your neighbor as yourself.

Romans 13:9 NIV

INTRODUCTION

Scripture tells us to "love our neighbor." How do we do that? In present day society, the word "love" brings images to our minds of romantic and/or friendly feelings. We see "love" portrayed on movie screens as fluttering eyelashes, stomach butterflies, wedding dresses, and Valentine chocolates. But true love—*biblical love*—has nothing to do with *feelings*. Biblical love is a *verb*, not a *noun*. Scriptural love—the kind Jesus refers to—is based on *what we do*, not on *what we feel*. Jesus' love allows us to love and help the unloved and unlovely in our world. We reach out to hurting people because, as Christians saved by grace through Jesus Christ, our love for God compels us to put our love into action.

We live in a world of hurting people. In this book, we will look primarily at how Christian women can reach out to wounded women as spiritual sisters who love them and care about them. This book is about real women with real problems. Women today endure many of the same unkind and harsh circumstances the women in Jesus' day suffered. In my own theology study, and after decades of working with wounded women, I have discovered that women suffer from a number of issues, including broken relationships and divorce; unforgiveness and bitterness; loneliness and discouragement; spouse abuse; childhood sexual abuse; children who complete suicide; and loss and grief. These are the issues we will study in this book.

How can we, as concerned spiritual sisters, reach out to our world's wounded women? We can reach out in the same ways Jesus Himself reached out to hurting women in his day. By following his example, we, too, can help women who suffer.

I have designed this book as a Bible study. It is a biblically-based study written especially for Christian women today. The purpose of this book is to show Christian women the vast need for service in our world, and to teach biblical ways to reach out in Christ's love to women who hurt. It is written for women of all evangelical denominations, all ages and all walks of life. The Bible Study Section at the end of the book can be used as a personal study for reflection and prayer, or as a group study.

My personal prayer is that *I Am My Sister's Keeper* will be a tool through which God can speak to you. May it touch your hearts and encourage you—as a spiritual sister—to reach out to the world's wounded women in Christ's name.

1

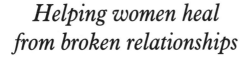

with God's truth

Helping women heal
from broken relationships

| Bible Study: Read John 4:4-42 |

The townswomen of Sychar must have gossiped about her behind her back. In the early mornings, when they filled their water jars at the local well, she may have hidden inside her home to avoid them. No woman in Sychar filled her jars at noon, in the extreme Middle East heat of the day. That is, except the wounded woman—a worn middle-aged woman with a sad, bitter heart. She came to the well for water during the hottest hour of the day. She surely longed to avoid the townswomen's accusing eyes, their critical comments, and their heads shaking at her in disgust. In those days, a husband could divorce a wife with just a word or a note written down and it could be for any reason or no reason at all.

We can read between the lines, as we study her story, found in John 4:4-42. We can imagine that five husbands used her up and then ran off. Maybe they grew tired of her and wanted younger, unused women. Maybe her face had wrinkled, her body sagged, her back bowed, and the husbands wanted fresh, pretty women. Who knows why five men used, and no doubt, abused her and then tossed her aside?

We meet this tired woman—a person we know only as the "Samaritan woman" – as she lugs her water jar to Jacob's well. The sun blazes overhead. Sweat pours from her face. Jacob's well has long been deserted by her female neighbors.

She thinks she's alone as she walks toward the well to fill her empty jug with water. But she's not alone. Jesus waits for her at Jacob's well. He, too, is tired and needs to sit down and rest. John tells us Jesus *"had to go through Samaria."* (v. 4). "Had to"? Yes, he "had to go." Not because geography dictated his traveling in that direction, but because he had a divine appointment with the woman at the well at noon. When she approaches the well, Jesus speaks to her directly.

Perhaps he startles her when he asks: "Will you give me a drink?" (v. 7).

"Oh, no! Another man!" she might have thought. "They all seem to want something from me! Why can't they just leave me alone?!"

She, no doubt, also wondered: "Why is this Jew speaking to me, a Samaritan? Why is this man speaking to me, a female? And why is this Jewish man speaking to me, a woman with a bad reputation? Doesn't he know the 'rules'? Doesn't he care anything about 'social appropriateness'?"

(Even Jesus' own disciples would later silently wonder about Jesus' "political correctness" in speaking to this Samaritan woman: "[His disciples] were surprised to find him talking with a woman." [v. 27]. But they dared not question or lecture Jesus.)

"You are a Jew and I am a Samaritan woman," she probably blurted out at him. "How can you ask me for a drink?"

Jews had rejected Samaritans due to their mixed Gentile blood and their differing style of worship.

But maybe something in Jesus' voice, his kindness, his tenderness, made her stop, look into his eyes, and dip him a cup of water. He spoke to her not as a harsh, critical townsman, but as a loving father might speak to a cherished daughter. Perhaps she heard the deep compassion in his voice, the note of caring, and understood he wasn't a "taker," like other men she had known. He was a "giver."

Every time I read her story, I want to reach into Scripture, shake this woman by the shoulders, and shout: "Woman from Samaria! Do you know who you are talking to?! It's God himself, coming to meet you in your own environment! Listen to him! Drink the living water he offers you! He can change your sad and messed-up life!"

She tests Jesus by playing some verbal games as she tries to figure him out. She finds excuses to prevent Jesus from probing too deeply into her inner world, her sinful lifestyle choices.

"You have nothing to draw with and the well is deep," she said. "Where can you get this living water?"

"Are you greater than our father Jacob, who gave us the well and drank from it himself, as did also his sons and his flocks and herds?" she said.

"Sir, give me this water so that I won't get thirsty and have to keep coming here to draw water," she told Jesus.

She still didn't understand.

She proved a hard woman, who trusted few people. Jesus must prove Himself to her. He continues with patience: "Go," Jesus says, "call your husband and come back."

"I have no husband!" she tells Him. At least she is honest with Jesus.

Jesus looks at this woman and He knows her – her heart, her past, and her present. "You are right when you say you have no husband. The fact is, you have had five husbands, and the man you now have is not your husband. What you have just said is quite true."

But she doesn't understand. Not yet. "Sir, I can see that you are a prophet. Our fathers worshiped on this mountain [Mount Gerizim], but you Jews claim that the place where we must worship is in Jerusalem."

She avoids the condition of her heart and conceals deep intimate conversation with needless words.

"I know that Messiah is coming," she tells him. "When he comes, he will explain everything to us."

Jesus interrupts the chatter and speaks directly to her: "I who speak to you am he." Jesus revealed the true worship of God to this woman that day. He showed her that He was this new location for worship of God the Father through Himself, God's Son.

The woman's eyes opened and she finally understood who Jesus was, and what he could do for her personally and eternally.

That day, Jesus reached out to a wounded woman with God's truth. He offered what only he could give her—living water to fill her empty heart, to nourish her suffering soul. The Savior's love replaced the bitterness in her heart. Jesus gave her a new life brimming with love and forgiveness and purpose.

She drank deeply from Jesus' cup that day—his cup of forgiveness. Jesus forgave her. Grace equipped her to forgive the townspeople who may have used, abused, and despised her. She must have forgiven them completely because she ran back to town and told them all about the saving Messiah and the living water he gave. She knew that they, too, needed to drink from the cup of forgiveness and salvation. That they, too, had bitter, unforgiving, and lost hearts. That they, too, had a desperate thirst that only Jesus could quench.

I like to think she forgave the five husbands who used her and tossed her aside. If she could speak to me right now from the Bible's pages, she might say something like this: "How can my heart hold bitterness now when Christ has so freely given me a beautiful new life, and has forgiven and forgotten my wicked, sinful past? I must forgive them because the Messiah has so forgiven me."

The woman became an early missionary. She forgot her water jar at the well, and she ran back to town. "Come," she called to the townspeople who despised her, who made her life so miserable. "Come see a man who told me everything I ever did. Could this be the Christ?!"

John tells us the townspeople came to the well to meet Jesus for themselves. He also states "many of the Samaritans from that town believed in him because of the woman's testimony." (v. 39). After meeting Jesus, they proclaimed: "…We know that this man really is the Savior of the world!" (v. 42).

They refused to let Jesus leave, and urged him to stay with them. Jesus spent several days with the people, no doubt answering their questions, teaching, preaching, praying with them, and filling their empty hearts with living water.

THE SADNESS OF DIVORCE

Life is made up of relationships. Since humans are imperfect creatures, forgiveness plays an essential role in life's journey as we strive to relate to others. How can we forgive fully, completely as Christ has forgiven us when we are faced with wrongs done against us? Many of these wrongs are so horrible, we might even consider them "un-forgive-able."

I've met and spoken with so many women who married hateful, abusive men. They cry, pray, and endure day after day with unkindness, with critical words hurled at them, with threats of divorce. Severing marriage ties can devastate a woman. Not only can she be destroyed emotionally by the loss of his love, but every part of her life may suffer as a result of divorce. Finances may plummet, and she may be unable to afford the food, shelter, and other necessities of life. She may become the sole support of their children, as well as the child's only parental advocate, spiritual leader, emotional-nurturer. She may painfully watch her children miss their daddy, wonder why he doesn't come home, and even blame themselves for his departure. Children are hurt by divorce—the death of a marriage, the death of a family's future together. We are saddened as a Christian community, but no longer shocked, when we hear that friends, acquaintances, neighbors, and fellow church members are filing for divorce. It happens so often these days—in our families and in our churches. In fact, I was shocked to discover that the divorce rates in Christian, church-going families are the same as in secular, un-churched, non-believers' marriages! In fact, some experts, who study the problem of divorce, say that the Christians' divorce rates are actually higher than the non-believers' divorce rates!

When a woman is rejected, shoved aside, and legally divorced, she may never recover from the pain, sadness, and embarrassment. She may lose all the friends she and her husband made together. She may find little support from friends or family when she's suddenly left alone. It's a sad situation, and the statistics just in the United States are frightening:

Two-thirds of all first marriages probably will end in separation or divorce.

Seventy-five percent of second marriages fail (*Marriage Savers*).

One million American children will see their parents divorce this year (*Marriage Savers*).

Other countries around the world are also dealing with high divorce rates. One study shows Sweden, Belarus, Finland, Luxembourg, Estonia, and Australia have more divorces than the United States. Running neck to neck with about the same number of divorces as the U.S. are Denmark, Belgium, Austria, Czech Republic, Russia, United Kingdom, Norway, Ukraine, and Iceland. What countries have the fewest divorces? According to this study, India, Sri Lanka, Macedonia, Bosnia, Herzegovina, Turkey, Armenia, and Georgia have very low divorce rates.[1]

Not only is divorce a world-wide problem, but it's also an age-old problem. In the first century A.D., Josephus and Philo, both ancient Jewish writers, explain that a man can divorce his wife for whatever cause. Some husbands divorced their wives because they burned and spoiled his supper, or because he found someone he liked better than his wife.[2] Women in those days had little security in a lasting marriage.

In Roman society at that time, a couple could divorce by simply considering themselves "no longer married." In fact, a husband could decide he was "no longer married," without even consulting his wife.[3]

---

1   Found at: http://www.infoplease.com/ipa/A0200806.html. Accessed: 1/24/10.

2   Found at: http://www.wisereaction.org/ebooks/wenham_divorce_first. pdf. Accessed: 1/24/10.

3   Found at: http://news.stanford.edu/pr/91/911203Arc1041.html. Accessed: 1/24/10.

SUSAN'S STORY

Let me tell you about my friend Susan. Susan married Wayne, a successful surgeon, twenty-six years ago. She loved him and dedicated herself to him. She supported and encouraged him through long years of medical school. She gave up her own dreams of becoming a doctor to make his goal come true. She faithfully maintained their home, and became mother to their two children. She never thought much about giving up her own career dreams, and gave herself fully to the role of Christian wife and mother.

During the first half of their marriage, Wayne and Susan both worked hard to support themselves and to pay Wayne's expensive medical-school tuition. They had little money to live on, and refinished yard-sale furniture for their tiny, two-room apartment. They also ate a lot of canned beans because they couldn't afford meat.

After Wayne finally graduated, he found a good-paying position in an out-of-state hospital. They moved out of their apartment, said goodbye to their friends, and bought their first house near the hospital. They enrolled their daughter in a nearby elementary school, and their son began kindergarten.

After Wayne's long struggle through school, Susan looked forward to a hopeful future with her husband and children. "Finally," she told a friend. "We can settle down, raise our children, and afford to pay our bills."

But then…you guessed it. It's becoming an all too familiar story these days. Wayne met an attractive young nurse at the hospital, and he told Susan he wanted a divorce. Susan deeply loved Wayne. But she also knew that Wayne no longer loved her, and he wanted to dissolve their marriage vows. She refused to hold onto a man who didn't want her anymore. But, the divorce broke Susan's heart.

Susan thought divorce was the last thing that could ever happen to her. It caught her totally off guard. Like many other women around the world, Susan found herself alone, the sole support for her two children, and hurting financially and emotionally.

"I felt so afraid," Susan said. "I didn't know if I could make it on my own."

Susan also felt intense hatred for Wayne, the man she once so deeply loved. "I hated him, and his new wife and family," she admitted. Bitterness and resentment rooted itself in Susan's heart. She moved out of their new home and back into a small affordable apartment. Then she began the long process of pulling her life back together and dealing with her hurt.

THE MARRIAGE RELATIONSHIP

God created humans to be in relationship with one another. In too many marriages, however, harmony in relationship is the exception, not the rule. The closer the relationship with another, the more fertile the breeding ground for conflict. The paradox is that the closer the relationship, the easier it should be to resolve conflict, right wrongs, and overcome hurts. When we are intimate with another person as in a marriage relationship, we are extremely open and vulnerable. We also should know that person like we know no other, and practice unconditional love and forgiveness.

Unfortunately, as in Susan's case, the most significant and humiliating pain seemed to occur in marriage—the one relationship that should have offered her the greatest security, happiness, and fulfillment.

The closeness of a marriage partnership, built on mutual trust and love, intensifies the hurt when separation occurs. When the one with whom a woman is most intimate chooses to end the relationship, the union, Susan, like many other women, are most often left confused, devastated, and bitter.

Many women feel they could more easily cope with the death of a spouse than with the pain caused by the loss of a husband through abandonment and/or divorce. In abandonment or divorce, women are not only left hurting by grief and loss, but often suffer a severe blow to their self-esteem. Yet they must continue to deal with their hurt while relating to the ex-spouse in child support, custody, and visitation agreements. In addition, Christians—the ones who should most readily forgive—often turn away, not quite knowing how to show the love and support these women so desperately need.

In my book, *What Women Wish Pastors Knew*, one newly-divorced woman with two sons told me that she had received little love and encouragement from her church and friends after her husband left her. "Had my husband died, instead of 'run off,' the church would have gathered around me, and shown me love and support. But, as a divorced woman, church members and friends almost completely ignored me. I was hurting as much as the widow. We had both lost a husband!"

Women need "spiritual sisters" when they face abandonment or divorce. God created women with relational natures. Loving friendships bring most women great fulfillment, satisfaction, and joy. Women share more than conversation and ideas and thoughts with each other. They often share their very hearts.

Oftentimes, however, women devastated by divorce close their hearts, even to their dearest female friends. When a Christian friend suggested that Susan needed to forgive Wayne, Susan lashed out at her.

"Put yourself in my place!" she told her friend. "Could you forgive Wayne if he had been your husband and the father of your children?

"Could you forgive Wayne while you watched him give Hawaiian vacations, expensive clothes, and a dream house to his new wife while you struggle to keep your son and daughter in shoes that fit?

"Could you forgive Wayne knowing that he was loving, providing for, and rearing his new wife's children after deliberately abandoning his own children?

"Could you invest twenty-six years of your life with Wayne, give up your own career dreams so he could achieve his dreams, and then so easily just forgive him?

"Could you truly let go of the bitterness and resentment you feel and forgive Wayne, knowing that forgiving him would mean forgiving the pain he caused you, and blocking from your mind the way he hurt you and the children?"

The wound proved too new, too raw, for Susan to accept her friend's love and advice to forgive Wayne.

Sometimes, as our "sister's keeper," we offer, in love, our ear. We listen and pray, and not so readily give our advice – even though we are right on target. Susan wasn't lashing out at her friend personally. She was still so filled with pain and disappointment at her husband's public rejection, she lashed out at the situation, not her spiritual sister.

TRUE FORGIVENESS: IS IT POSSIBLE?

Perhaps you've been hurt by a husband's actions— abandoned, divorced, or mistreated in some way. You might believe that forgiving your husband for the wrong done against you is just not humanly possible.

Forgiveness is a mystery, a process we cannot understand, a gift from God given freely to us. Forgiveness is not a three-step, ten-step, or twelve-step program. Forgiveness does not come naturally to us. Our natural tendency is to get even. Revenge, not unlimited pardon, is our common human instinct.

As a world society, we believe if he hits you, punch him back.

If she curses you, curse her back.

We do this "natural thing" of seeking revenge person to person, family to family, and nation to nation. It's the way our world lives in relationship with one another. "Eye for an eye; tooth for a tooth." Turn the other cheek? Not on your life!

But God expects us to take a route opposite the "get even" road of revenge. He tells us to forgive and to love. He shows us the other way to live. And surely, God's love is stronger than our basic instinct for revenge.

No doubt, you have met women who have been hurt by divorce, abandonment, and rejection. Perhaps you too are among the hurting. Bitterness so often accompanies divorce, abandonment, and rejection that forgiveness seems impossible. But forgiveness is essential for healing the hurt, for draining the bitterness, for beginning life with new purpose. You and I must share with our hurting sisters that, by God's grace, they can make the decision to forgive a rejecting husband. When the time is right, and our sister is ready to hear us, we can encourage her with God's Word about forgiveness, pray with her, and lovingly help her decide to forgive. We can't expect complete forgiveness to happen overnight. It sometimes takes a long time to complete that difficult journey. But she can make the decision to forgive him, and allow God to help her through the process.

WOULDN'T IT BE EASIER NOT TO FORGIVE?

Yes, deciding not to forgive might be the easy route, but it certainly isn't the right route. Why forgive someone who purposely causes you pain? Some people claim that:

- forgiving makes us better persons
- forgiving makes us feel good inside
- forgiving reduces our stress levels

Maybe this is true for some people. But for Christian women, we forgive because Jesus tells us to forgive! If for no other reason, that's why we should forgive our offender. Jesus said; "You have heard that it was said, 'You shall love your neighbor and hate your enemy.' But I say to you, love your enemies and pray for those who persecute you" (Matt. 5:43-44 RSV).

Paul wrote to the Colossians: "Bear with each other and forgive whatever grievances you may have against one another. Forgive as the Lord forgave you." (Col. 3:13).

Jesus told Peter to forgive his erring brother seventy times seven (see Matt. 18:21-35).

Those were radical words to the people of Jesus' day. And to many Christians, they seem like radical words today.

IF GOD CAN FORGIVE US…

If God can wipe clean our sin-scribbled slate, then how, as women in Christ, can we live with unforgiving spirits toward our brothers and sisters? Nothing will weigh us down in our Christian walk like unresolved anger, bitterness, and resentment. If we are to continue the marathon of life, we must "lay aside every weight" (Heb. 12:1 KJV).

As spiritual sisters, we need to explain to the hurting women around us that forgiveness does not necessarily involve how we feel toward persons we forgive. We may not want to resume friendships with people who hurt us. We can love the person in Christ and still not especially like them or their individual characteristics and ways of relating. The way we feel has little to do with extending the gift of forgiveness. Thank goodness!

Forgiveness is a decision we make, an act of the will. We decide to forgive and then we ask God, through his forgiveness for us, to enable us to forgive the one who has hurt us. We do not forgive in our own strength. We forgive through God's strength. Without God's grace, true forgiveness is not possible.

"We have the capacity to forgive when we have been deeply hurt because Christ within us is able to release forgiveness toward anyone through us. ... As we forgive one another, we release ourselves from bitterness."[4]

RELEASING THE DEBT

For two years after Wayne divorced Susan, she was an emotional wreck.

"I felt intense anger and suffered from deep depression," Susan said. "I remember one morning kneeling by my bed and praying. My clothes were spread out in front of me, but I was so depressed I couldn't get dressed. I kept repeating to myself: 'Susan, all you have to do is just take off your nightgown and put on your shirt and jeans.' I was so drained of emotional energy, I was so depressed, I sat on the floor for thirty minutes trying to perform the simple task of getting dressed."

Susan sought the help of a good Christian counselor and several close Christian friends. She decided to forgive Wayne, to release him from the debt of hurting her.

"When I looked in the mirror, I saw a bitter 45-year-old woman staring back at me," she remembers.

---

4   Charles Stanley, *Forgiveness* (Nashville: Thomas Nelson, Inc., 1987), pp. 168-9.

"And I told myself: 'Susan, you're a bitter young woman, and one of these days you will be a bitter old woman if you don't forgive Wayne and start to heal.' The last thing in the world I wanted to be was a bitter old woman!"

Susan still felt the pain of betrayal and rejection, but she prayed that God would enable her to make the decision to forgive Wayne.

"I couldn't do it on my own," she recalls. "It was God in me that forgave Wayne. I also prayed that God would release me from the bitterness and resentment I felt toward Wayne and his new wife. I couldn't do that on my own either. But I have discovered that God is the God of miracles, and He certainly worked the miracle of forgiveness in my life."

Not long after she forgave Wayne, Susan began to heal. Today she is a happy, vibrant woman who is a joy to be around, a devoted churchwoman who actively reaches out to other women suffering the trauma of divorce. She is a woman with new determination, and new purpose.

MISCONCEPTIONS ABOUT FORGIVENESS

Some women believe that if they wait long enough, time will heal them. But time is usually an enemy. Not a friend. When a woman harbors an unforgiving spirit, time can increase the hate, bitterness, and resentment she can feel. Hate, then, becomes a way of life, a burden to bear, a way of relating that becomes the woman's very identity. Year after year, some women hold on tightly to their hurts and resentments. Their painful pasts color everything they see, think, and do, every experience they have. Hurts continue to grow, overwhelming them until life becomes a painful moment by moment ritual.

Another misconception about forgiveness is that we must understand the whole painful situation or the offender's reason before we can forgive. We falsely think we must carefully and painstakingly analyze, scrutinize, digest, and re-digest the angry words, the mean attitudes, the cruel actions, and the intended meanings before we can forgive and begin to heal.

At first, Susan thought full-time about the injustices her husband heaped upon her. She could not get his rejecting and hateful behavior off her mind. It kept her from sleeping at night. The knot in her stomach kept her from eating. She analyzed every word she remembered when he told her he wanted a divorce. She thought back again and again on their life together, and tried to figure out what went wrong.

A Christian woman told Susan: "Susan, you don't have to understand to accept a painful situation. And we don't have to understand to forgive the one who has so hurt us. Through Christ, we can extend the gift of a second chance, and our hearts can be bathed in cleansing forgiveness without understanding all the details of the painful transaction."

Her advice helped Susan. Susan never understood why Wayne deliberately hurt her, rejected her, and ended their marriage. But she forgave Wayne anyway, without understanding everything that went wrong and why it went wrong. Wayne also never apologized to Susan for leaving her and the children. Nor did he ever ask Susan for forgiveness. Apologies are nice when they happen, but they aren't necessary to complete forgiveness. Through God's grace, as Susan had been forgiven by God, she chose to forgive Wayne.

Susan made the decision to forgive Wayne. Then she asked God for insight and understanding later. She allowed healing to begin in her heart and soul before she had a clear understanding of Wayne's behavior and actions. By forgiving, Susan stated to God that she accepted God's plan for her life, and that she aimed to become more Christ-like with every new day.

Susan also came to understand that forgiveness does not necessarily include reconciliation. It was not possible for Wayne and Susan to get back together or to remarry. Wayne had already married another woman and had fathered her children. Forgiveness doesn't depend on reconciliation or reunion. Surely, complete reconciliation is a future happening that God will arrange in his own way. Our job is to forgive and leave the rest to God.

Let's talk for a minute about what happens when a Christian woman chooses to live with an unforgiving spirit.

Forgiveness is putting into practice what we believe about God's love and grace. God's Word becomes more real to us when we use it within the daily context of our lives. Only because of God's unconditional love for us can we accept and forgive others with a love unconditional to, and in spite of, someone's intentional injuries to us.

This type of rare, unconditional love comes only from God. It covers a multitude of evils heaped upon us by others. It covers rejecting spouses, and also betraying friends, and abusive parents. It covers gossiping townspeople who give unkind looks and shake their heads in disgust. It covers those who promise to "love and honor" till death parts them, and then break that vow and walk away.

GOD'S HEALING

God provides healing for the injustices and tragedies of life. Nothing or no one can be the *source* of this healing; it comes only from God. But we can be an *agent* of God's healing.

Paul wrote: "Be kind and compassionate to one another, forgiving each other, just as in Christ God forgave you." (Eph. 4:32).

As our sisters' keeper, let us help those women around us who have been deeply hurt, to live in Christ's **forgiving** spirit, so that it becomes a way of life for them. Surely, this is the life God calls women to live.

2

REACHING

with forgiveness

OUT

- Helping women forgive themselves

| Bible Study: Read John 8:1-11 |

She was guilty of sin. Caught in the act of adultery, the law condemned her to death by stoning. With rocks clenched in their fists, the zealous religious leaders waited impatiently as they tested Jesus. Would Jesus obey Israel's covenant law? Or would Jesus show the sinful woman mercy? Jesus stood there, trapped between his allegiance to the law and his merciful love for those who violated the law.

You know the rest of the story. Each man dropped his stone, one by one. Each man knew that he, too, had broken the law of Moses. He knew that he had a sinful heart and that he deserved the sentence of death.

What about the woman we know only as the "adulteress"? She walked away untouched by the rocks of punishment. Jesus forgave her. He set her free.

But I wonder: Did this woman ever forgive herself for her wrong-doing? Jesus had forgiven her and set her free from her sins. She no longer had to carry the heavy burden of her past. Jesus now carried it for her. He freed her from her burden.

Jesus continues to free women from the burden of sin, yet many of them refuse to forgive themselves. They continue to condemn themselves and cause themselves great pain. Often the same women will reach out in forgiveness to those who have hurt them deeply, yet keep the pain fresh in their hearts because they fail to release themselves from their God-forgiven debts.

How Can We Forgive Ourselves?

Our failure to forgive ourselves can be devastating. Day after day, it consumes body, mind, and emotions. Slowly it destroys. Our churches and communities are filled with women who are hurt by their misunderstanding of Scripture and their misunderstanding of God's redeeming love. They are the women God has forgiven, and who have forgiven those who have hurt them—but they cannot forgive themselves. How desperately they need to hear the message from you!

If they have accepted God's forgiveness, if they have made the decision to forgive others, then they must also learn to forgive themselves completely.

Otherwise, they cannot find healing; they cannot be completely whole. A shadow lurks behind them everywhere they go. They carry heavy baggage on their shoulders, and refuse to put the load down and find relief.

A forgiven, forgiving, cleansed heart is the only kind of heart God can use in his service. A heart filled with bitterness, resentment, and hatred toward God, others, or oneself is a heart with little room left for love. A burdened heart cannot fully reach out and help others.

Before we approach these women with the message, however, let us examine our own hearts. How can we reach out to others who have stumbled and fallen if we, ourselves, have heavy, unforgiving hearts?

Jesus came, and he died on the cross to reconcile us to God. We call it "atonement," for in his death we find "at-one-ment" with God. As believers, we are made right with God.

Jesus Christ is the source of forgiveness. We often accept his forgiveness and forgive those who have wronged us, but we can so often fail to forgive ourselves.

We must learn to forgive ourselves. If we choose not to, we will live a life of sadness, our usefulness to God and to others needlessly hindered or sacrificed. We will live a life void of joy and purpose.

In Jeremiah 31:34, God promised to forgive our sins and remember them no more. In our finite minds we wonder how a God so powerful, so all-knowing, could forget anything. God knows the number of hairs on our heads, and he knows our thoughts before we think them. God knows everything we have done and ever will do.

How could God "forget"? Because God, in his infinite wisdom, *chooses* to forget. God makes a choice that what we have done will have no effect on the way he responds in mercy.

Christ died for the forgiveness of our sins—past, present, and future. Nothing we have done is beyond the reach of God's love and power to forgive.

THE PRODIGAL DAUGHTER

I met Iris Blue when she came to my church in Birmingham, Alabama, to speak. Her story is amazing.

Iris Blue's problems began about the time she was born. She can laugh about those early years now.

"I had a problem," she jokes. "I was born big! I was so big that, in elementary school, the teachers would raise their hands and ask me for permission to go to the bathroom! When I started to like boys, I would lean up against the school locker and try to look sexy. The locker would cave in!"

Iris can joke about her past now. But not so long ago, Iris's life wasn't so funny.

In a more serious tone, Iris reflects: "I really liked boys, and I wanted them to notice me."

But Iris had seen the kind of girls that got the boys' attention, the tall, skinny, beautiful women that adorned billboards and beauty pageant stages. She knew she could never fit into those size 5 Cinderella shoes.

"At an early, early age," Iris recalls, "I had a dream. I wanted to be a lady. I wanted to be gracious and kind, a wife and mother with a family and home. I just wanted to be *a lady*."

One day Iris asked her mother why she was so big. Her mother told her that God did that to her. That upset Iris. She felt like God had started making a football player and then changed his mind. "And then I found out that the football players' 'shoulders' came off at night," she quips. "Mine didn't!"

Iris was rebellious. When she was a young girl, she ran away from home. Within weeks of the first time she ran away, she got involved in drugs. Within days after that, she was involved in things she never dreamed she'd be involved in—bars, topless clubs, and other things.

"I ended up in bad shape," she remembers. "I was strung out on heroin, and I started stealing every day. When I got caught, my mother and dad would cry, and I'd make big promises to change." Iris wanted to keep her promises, but she didn't.

By age seventeen, Iris had been arrested several times, the last time for armed robbery. She remained in jail nine months before being sentenced to eight years in prison. During those years, Iris stayed in constant trouble, and in and out of the hospital trying to kick her drug habit. Due to her arrogant, rebellious behavior, she spent most of her prison time in solitary confinement.

"I cussed, swore, and hit the prison matrons. I ended up being locked in the basement of the prison."

In the dark prison basement, Iris had time to think about her life. "My past was so full of guilt I couldn't handle it. I didn't want to think about my present condition. And I sure didn't want to think about the future because anybody with any sense knew I'd be an uneducated, ex-convict with a smart mouth. I knew I wouldn't have much chance in life even if I got out of prison.

Iris had lost hope in herself. She carried on her shoulders the heavy bag of unforgiven sin. She could not shake it off.

"In the privacy of that cell where nobody could see me, I fantasized my life away. I used to pretend I was a lady, pretty and feminine."

Iris served her full sentence in prison. When she was released back into society, she had not changed. She was still bitter and angry. Before long, she was back on drugs, back in the bars, and running a topless nightclub.

Then, remarkably, came her turning point.

A young Christian man came into the nightclub one night to share his newfound faith. He told Iris that Jesus loved her. But she wasn't interested. He called, visited, and continued to witness to her, but she didn't listen. Finally, he was advised by a minister friend to leave her alone. His friend feared that Iris might influence the young Christian man with her evil ways.

When he told Iris he wouldn't be coming back, she finally listened to him. "I can't be around an old tramp like you anymore!" he told her. Then he added: "You don't even know that Jesus Christ could make you a lady!"

Those words touched Iris's hard heart. She will never forget how she felt when she heard his comment.

"My heart just ripped apart," she said. "I had gone down a long road looking in a lot of directions. But that's all I had ever really wanted—just to be a lady."

"Jesus could do that, he told me. He could take an old tramp like me and make her a lady."

Suddenly, Iris felt her heart start to soften. He had spoken the words she had long dreamed about coming true.

"A lady?" she asked him, and then added: "I want that. Whatever it takes, I'm ready."

Together they went outside, away from the blaring music and flashing lights, away from the dancers in the windows. "I knelt down by the car out front," Iris remembers. "I knelt down and I prayed."

That night, God worked a miracle in Iris Blue's life when she knelt down, confessed her many sins, and asked Christ to come into her heart and forgive her. She gave complete control of her life to Jesus Christ, and Christ changed her. He changed her heart, her attitude, and her life. Forever.

Through his gift of forgiveness, Christ gave Iris a new life, cleansed and pure. He gave her purpose, a new beginning, a second chance.

He made her his daughter—brought her into God's own family—and through the power of the Holy Spirit, he helped her to forgive herself of her depraved past.

"That night," Iris Blue remembers, "I knelt down a tramp by that car and prayed, but I stood up a *lady*."

Just imagine if that persistent young Christian man had given up, or said that Iris's life was an impossible one to save. Where would Iris be today? He was "his sister's keeper," and God used him to bring Iris into his fold.[1]

WHEN WE FAIL

If Christ can forgive us of our many sins, why do we find it so difficult to forgive ourselves? It seems much easier to forgive others who hurt us, than to forgive ourselves when we make a mistake or fail at something.

Paul said: "There is therefore now no condemnation for those who are in Christ Jesus" (Rom. 8:1). No Christian needs to experience unforgiveness of her own wrong-doings. No Christian needs to carry guilt around with her when God forgives her.

Guilt. The apostle Paul knew about guilt. Before his unforgettable experience on the road to Damascus, Paul was named Saul. He was a religious fanatic—a Pharisee—trying his best to stomp out first century Christianity single-handedly. He was a Christian-killer, and everyone knew him by that reputation. He lived in a violent society that applauded the killing of Christians. And he was a citizen of the official Roman Empire, and that gave him credentials and prestige.

He went about his murdering task with great enthusiasm and fervor. That is, until he met Jesus Christ in his travels on the road to Damascus.

God had to knock Saul off his horse and blind his eyes, to get the man's attention. But, in doing so, Christ changed Saul's murderous heart. Saul, turned Paul, became one of the greatest missionaries the world has ever known.

---

1   Iris Blue's story used by permission—from *Iris Blue*.

Paul accepted Christ's forgiveness for the horrible things he had personally done. But did Paul ever forgive himself for the havoc and horror he had caused Christ's followers?

Fortunately, Scripture tells us that answer. Yes, Paul forgave himself. He stood before the council and the high priest Ananias, and said with all honesty: "Brethren, I have lived before God in all good conscience up to this day" (Acts 23:1 RSV).

In saying that, we can be certain that Paul accepted Jesus' forgiveness of his many sins, and he also forgave himself. Scripture reveals that Paul was able to forgive himself completely for his past. He stood before the Lord and the Sanhedrin with a clear conscience. Forgiven. The heavy bag of burdensome guilt fell off his shoulders. God gave him a clean conscience, a "good conscience," and Paul put the past behind him and carried forth from that day God's purpose.

And what about the Old Testament's King David? He stole another man's wife, who, incidentally, became pregnant from the encounter. Then he had her husband, Uriah, killed on the battlefield. Can God forgive that kind of "trespass"?

Yes, God forgave David. But could David forgive himself after that?

Listen to David's prayer for healing and moral restoration in Psalm 51:

"Have mercy on me, O God, according to thy steadfast love; according to thy abundant mercy blot out my transgressions. Wash me thoroughly from my iniquity, and cleanse me from my sin! For I know my transgressions, and my sin is ever before me. Purge me with hyssop, and I shall be whiter than snow. Fill me with joy and gladness … Create in me a clean heart, O God, and put a new and right spirit within me. … Restore to me the joy of thy salvation. … Deliver me from blood-guiltiness, O God, … and my tongue will sing aloud of thy deliverance. … A broken and contrite heart, O God, thou wilt not despise" (Ps. 51:1-3, 7, 8, 10, 12, 14, 17 RSV).

In his prayer, David uses the imagery of bathing—"wash me," "cleanse me," "purge me with hyssop." In those days, people used the plant hyssop for cleansing and in religious purification services.[2] David begged God to clean up his heart, to restore the joy he knew before he sinned, to deliver him from the "blood on his hands"—the selfish murder of Uriah. He comes to God, the Forgiver, with a broken heart, a heart that desperately needs cleansing and restoration.

Even after all he had done, after David's prayer for forgiveness, he could talk of "cleansing," "a clean heart," a "new and right spirit," "deliverance," and of being once again filled with "joy and gladness." Only after he had been forgiven by God and only after God had enabled him to forgive himself could King David ask God: "Restore to me the joy of thy salvation" (v. 12). Later, a completely forgiven David, with clear conscience, could write:

"My whole being, praise the Lord … The Lord forgives me for all my sins … He loads me with love and mercy. He satisfies me with good things. He makes me young again, like the eagle … As high

2   Found at: http://www.bible-history.com/smiths/H/Hyssop/. Accessed: 1/25/10.

as the sky is above the earth, so great is his love for those who respect him. He has taken our sins away from us as far as the east is from west ... He knows how we were made. He remembers that we are dust" (Ps. 103:1, 3-5, 11, 12, 13 NCV).

How interesting that David referred to God's removal of sin as far as the east is from west! Remember, in those days, people did not understand that the Earth was round. He could not know that his "east to west" analogy meant that God's forgiveness was like a circle—unending, but round and round again and again.

GOD'S FORGIVENESS

Not long ago, I spoke to a large group of women on the topic of forgiveness. I speak on forgiveness often around the United States and far off places, like Europe and Japan. A woman listened to me as I explained God's forgiveness and how he makes it possible for us to forgive ourselves.

"We must *choose* to forgive our *enemies*," I told the women. The woman stood up and made a comment that surprised me. "What if," she said, "That enemy I need to forgive—is *me*?"

Maybe you, too, are finding it difficult, or even impossible, to forgive yourself of a past sin. Perhaps you'd agree with this woman—you, yourself, are your worst enemy. Maybe you have a friend or family member who carries a bag of heavy guilt on her shoulders and can't put it down.

If so, know that God's incredible love covers a multitude of sins. We confess. He forgives. In fact, God forgives us before we even confess.

Charles Stanley writes: "Forgiveness is based on the atoning work of the Cross, and not on anything we do. God's forgiveness does not depend on our confession, nor does his fellowship.

"Confession is a means for releasing us from the tension and bondage of a guilty conscience. When we pray, 'God, you are right. I've sinned against you. I am guilty of this act. I am guilty of that thought,' we achieve release."[3]

Even before we confess our wrongs, God encircles us with his never-ending circle of forgiveness, east becoming west and west becoming east.

We must tell hurting women this: If you are a follower of Jesus Christ and have committed your life to Him, you can know without a doubt that God has forgiven your past, present, and future wrongdoings. However, if you are still struggling under the weight of a heavy load of guilt, know that you are carrying a burden God does not intend for you to carry.

Unfortunately, some Christian women carry a burden of guilt for a lifetime. They are wounded by self-induced sores of guilt that never heal. They just can't let go of them. They carry them around forever—needlessly. The sores cause them unceasing distress and pain. Sometimes they cover up their sores of guilt with busyness, interesting conversation, or the latest fashions or television movie. But, in the dark quiet of the night, in the still early moments of the morning, and during the times in their day when they pause to rest, they are once again aware of their wounds.

---

3   Charles Stanley, *Forgiveness* (Nashville: Oliver Nelson, 1987), p. 136.

We all sin. We all make mistakes, even the most dedicated Christian women; but that doesn't mean we are failures. It just means we are "human," we are "dust." That doesn't mean we must be stopped by our failures, never again to be used by God. Christ extends to us his hand of forgiveness, and he offers us the power and the gift of forgiving ourselves when we stumble and fall.

FORGIVEN AND FIT FOR MINISTRY

Having a purpose. Being used by God. That's what our Christian lives are all about, isn't it?

Today Iris Blue radiates Christ's love in her presence, her lifestyle, and her speech. She is happily married to a dedicated Christian man, Duane, and together they have a son, Denim. Iris and Duane travel in full-time ministry, speaking to churches, schools, and prisons, telling everyone what Jesus Christ has done for them and what he can do for all.

In many ways, the story of Iris Blue reminds me of the woman caught in adultery. This woman had a real problem. According to the law of Moses, if two eyewitnesses saw a woman in the act of adultery, the respectable people of the town could pick up rocks and stone her.

So the religious leaders tested Jesus. "What do you think, Jesus?" they asked. "Are we going to obey the law of Moses and kill her?"

Jesus didn't speak. Instead, he slowly knelt and wrote words on the ground. Mystery words. As far as we know, the only words Jesus ever wrote were these words he wrote on the ground.

Then he stood up and said to them: "Let him who is without sin among you be the first to throw a stone at her."

These "stones" weren't pebbles. They were huge boulders used to bash out her brains.

One by one, stones were dropped from sinful hands. The sound they made as they dropped one by one to the ground "spoke volumes."

Soon Jesus was left alone with the woman before him. Everyone else had deserted them.

Ken Gire paints a beautiful word picture in his book, *Intimate Moments with the Savior*:

"They are alone now—lawbreaker and lawgiver. And the only one qualified to condemn her, doesn't.

"She takes a deep breath. Her heart is a fluttering moth held captive in his hands.

"The Savior has stood up for this unknown woman and fought for her … He stands up again, this time to free her.

"'Has no one condemned you?' he asks.

"Timid words stumble from her lips, 'No one, sir.'

"What comes are words of grace, 'Neither do I condemn you….'

"… She looks into his face. His forehead relaxes. It has been an ordeal for him, too. He takes a breath and his smile seems to say 'Go, you're free now.'"[4]

THE MESSAGE JESUS GAVE HER
This story, and Jesus' words to both the religious leaders and the sinful woman, send a strong message

---

4   Ken Gire, *Intimate Moments with the Savior* (Grand Rapids: Zondervan Publishing House, 1989), pp. 57-8.

to us today: Don't judge others. Don't be eager to stand smugly pharisaic and bring to light another's faults, weaknesses, failures, and dirty laundry. After all, as Scripture tells us, it's difficult to pick out a splinter in your sister's eye when you're carrying a load of firewood in your own eye!

But there is another message in the story, too. Here is a woman who has been dragged through the dirt, proclaimed guilty by the local townspeople and religious leaders, and permanently branded as an adulteress. She thought she would be lying in the street by now, bleeding, dying. Instead, she has been given a new life, a second chance, a new beginning by the one called Jesus.

No doubt, she was forever shunned by the more "decent" townswomen and ridiculed and mocked by the temple leaders. She must have heard the laughter and whispers about her when she carried her water jars to the local well or shopped for food in the city's streets. She must have seen the city's "proper" women divert their eyes when she met them in the marketplace.

But after her encounter with Jesus, she was a daughter of the King! A forgiven daughter of the forgiving King. She had been cleansed, restored, and made whole by the King himself. In God's eyes her careless, sinful act of adultery had been forgiven. The woman was free from sin and guilt. And even with her depraved past, God, no doubt, had future plans for her in his divine work.

GOD'S PROMISES

God makes us a promise: "If we walk in the light as he himself is in the light, we have fellowship with one another, and the blood of Jesus His Son cleanses us from all sin. ... If we confess our sins, he is faithful and righteous to forgive us our sins and to cleanse us from all unrighteousness" (1 John 1:7, 9 NASB).

How sad it would be if the woman had gone back to her home, and for the remainder of her years, had beaten herself down emotionally and mentally for the wrongs that Jesus had forgiven and forgotten. How sad if the woman had become a person whose past sins, now forgiven, still made her feel dirty, unclean. What a waste of a life.

When we are forgiven by God, we are no longer condemned and sentenced to "guilty." How unfortunate if we allow guilt to cripple us for a lifetime, a lifetime that could be used serving God with joy, gladness, and purpose. Perhaps guilt is one of Satan's most potent tools.

"Develop a godly tenacity and keep following Christ. You may make mistakes, you may encounter others' disapproval, ... you occasionally may dishonor the Lord, ... but realize that you are deeply loved, completely forgiven, fully pleasing, totally accepted, and absolutely complete because Christ died for you and was raised from the dead to give you new life."[5]

WHATEVER HAPPENED TO THIS WOMAN?

We will never know what happened to the one we've come to know only as "the adulterous woman."

---

5   Gire, pp. 57-8

Perhaps in her old age, long after Jesus' death and resurrection, she took her daughters and her granddaughters to the place where, long ago, she had been condemned to die.

Although Scripture doesn't record it, let us try to imagine the possible scene.

"This is where the townspeople dragged me," she points her finger toward the town's main meeting square.

"And this is where Jesus stooped down and wrote on the ground," she tells them.

I can envision her daughters and granddaughters kneeling together, searching for a remnant trace of a letter written by Jesus' own hand.

"And this is where they threw me down, the place where I was to be stoned to death. But Jesus was standing there," she says softly and smiles as she remembers his kind face, his tender eyes. "And he took me by the hand, forgave me, and gave me a new life. A wonderfully-cleansed and restored new life.

"This is where I looked into my Savior's eyes, the place where He made me pure. And this is the place, right here, this very spot, where I was forgiven, where I stood up *a lady*."

3

REACHING

to others with prayer

OUT

Helping women cope with loneliness

| Bible Study: Read John 11:1-44 |

Jesus loved Mary, Martha, and Lazarus. When Lazarus became gravely ill, his sisters summoned Jesus to their side. But before Jesus arrived in Bethany, Lazarus had been dead and buried for four days.

In love and tenderness, Jesus reached out to the bereaved sisters. To Martha, he gave the good news of resurrection. She needed to hear that Jesus is the "resurrection and the life" (John 11:25). To Mary, he gave tenderness and joined her in mourning Lazarus' death. Jesus wept with her. And to Lazarus, Jesus reached out with a prayer powerful enough to raise the dead.

"Jesus looked up to heaven and said, 'Father, I thank you that you have heard me'" (v. 41).

After his prayer, Jesus turned toward the tomb.

"Lazarus, come out!" Jesus shouted to the man.

Lazarus looked like a mummy as he walked out from the tomb, still wrapped in funeral clothes from head to toe. But Lazarus was very much alive.

Prayer. Have you noticed that whenever the situation seemed hopeless, Jesus reached out with prayer? When 5,000 people were desperately hungry, Jesus held five loaves of bread and two fish in his hands, and looked toward heaven.

Mark tells us what happened: "[Jesus] gave thanks and broke the loaves" (Mark 6:41). He fed the whole crowd.

When Jesus anticipated his own death, he brought his disciples together in a room to eat their last supper with him. Jesus took the bread and wine and then prayed. He reached out to his disciples with the comfort of prayer (Mark 14:22-23). He knew they would need it during the next few days.

Scripture records one of Jesus' prayers in John 17. Jesus prayed not only for his disciples, who would face the greatest heartbreak of their lives, but for you and me. He reached out to comfort us with an eternal prayer.

"I pray also for those who will believe in me through their message, that all of them may be one, Father, just as you are in me and I am in you" (vv. 20, 21).

PRAYER: A PRIORITY

Jesus made prayer and fellowship with the Father the priority in his life. Whether Jesus reached out to heal a man born blind, lifted small children up onto his lap, or took a whip to the temple money changers, he knew that God was only a heart's whisper away. The Father and Son had unbroken communion throughout the days of Jesus' life on earth. Jesus kept his heart focused on his Father while he worked, traveled, and ministered.

It is no wonder that Jesus reached out with prayer to those who hurt. Prayer was a priority in his life. He lived it, breathed it, and shared it.

You and I can reach out to hurting women with prayer. We can share with them the promise that God is only a whisper away. The Father yearns for each of us to pray and seek his presence. God reaches out to his children with the gift of prayerful fellowship. Yet some Christian women live in despair and loneliness when God's fellowship lies within reach. You and I can tell hurting women today about the gift of prayer, the beauty of fellowship with the Father who loves them more than they will ever know.

MARY

One of the loneliest women I've ever met was Mary. I first met Mary on the beach. Awaiting the sunrise, I had walked miles that morning along the white sands of Gulf Shores, Alabama.

Like the first hints of sunlight suddenly piercing the dark sky, Mary seemed to appear from nowhere. A woman entering her autumn years, she brushed aside strands of hair from her softly lined face. Except for the movement of her hand, she stood very still. As if reminiscing, she focused her eyes on the distant horizon.

Alone on the beach, too early for vacationing crowds, our paths crossed, I believe by divine providence. We stopped to exchange a greeting.

"A beautiful day," I spoke softly against the backdrop of the docile, rolling whitecaps. "The sea is so calm and blue this morning."

"Yes," the stranger responded. "The water is resting and at peace now." She hesitated and bit her bottom lip lightly. "But sometimes," she continued, her eyes still searching the horizon, "the sea can be sad and gray."

I felt an inner tug at my heart as I listened to the deeper meaning of Mary's odd words. Mary wasn't talking about the sea at all. Mary was talking about herself.

Sensing a moment of openness and opportunity, I asked a question of the woman whose name I did not yet know. "You seem to be troubled. Can I help you?"

I prayed silently that God would allow me to see Mary's heart, that he would enable me to hear what he wanted me to hear, and show me how to reach out to her.

And he did. During the next few minutes, I felt God's presence move closer, filling our mouths, minds, and hearts with words usually reserved for longtime friends.

It was as if God told me: "Denise, stop talking. Just listen to Mary. She, herself, will tell you everything you need to know in order to reach out to her and minister. Just listen, Denise. Don't talk."

I listened carefully to what she said, and what she didn't say.

"I come every year now," she told me and rubbed her eye with the back of her hand. "I've come every year for ten years since my beloved husband died. We used to come here together to celebrate our wedding anniversary. I come now to celebrate and to remember our anniversary…alone."

Mary talked. I listened. I discovered Mary was very lonely, sad, and felt no one loved her or cared about her. She had outlived her husband and most of her family. Before we parted, Mary smiled. I'll never forget her last words to me before she and I went our separate ways back out into life.

"Denise," she told me, "Do you know what I miss most since my husband's death? I miss not being *number one* with anybody anymore. No one loves me like he loved me. I miss him so much."

Then her voice softened, and her next words touched my soul.

"My heart is broken," she whispered.

There, she said it. Now her heart and soul were opened so that she could listen to me. I prayed to God for the words to tell her, and I felt my eyes mist.

"Mary," I responded. "I, too, have been sad and lonely in my life. But, let me tell you what I discovered during those times. You're *number one* with God. God loves you more than anyone ever has or ever could love you. He loved you so much, he came, and he faced death so you could one day be with him for eternity. And if you'll let him, Mary, God will heal your broken heart."

For a long moment, Mary dropped her eyes. Then she smiled, squeezed my hand, and nodded goodbye.

A tiny seed planted. Just a kind, loving word to a broken-hearted stranger. *Will it grow and blossom and produce fruit?* I wondered. Only God knows.

Many lonely women walk white sandy beaches and feel alone, sad, and broken-hearted. They are everywhere. They constantly cross our paths. Sometimes we recognize their sadness. Most of the time, however, I don't think we "see" them in a deeper way so that we can reach out to help them. But when we see deeper than the outside appearance, when God sets his daughters directly in our path, we can plant seeds within hearts—and sometimes they take root and grow. Someone down the road may fertilize the tender seedling. Another person may slightly prune its leaves. Someone, somewhere, may harvest the fruit. But it takes a caring spiritual sister to plant the first small seed.

Every Christian woman must become a farmer! Women today are deeply hurting. Society places too many expectations on today's woman. Women carry too many responsibilities on their shoulders. Stress levels are high. And I don't see too many women handling the stress well. They fill the pews of our churches. We can become so busy handling our own expectations, responsibilities, and stress levels, that we have no time or energy to "see" and "hear" the hearts of most lonely women.

Before Mary walked away—never to again cross my path in this life—she turned her face toward the blue sea. As if pondering again its age-old mysteries, she took a deep breath and slowly exhaled.

I stood there silently and watched Mary walk slowly along the shoreline until I could no longer see her. Did my simple words make any difference to Mary? I wondered. I don't know. Maybe not. But I do know this—I had to say them. I had to say them because I **am** my sister's keeper.

Oh, how often has a spiritual sister come to me when I was down and lonely, and brought me comfort through God's Word. "Denise, don't you know that the Lord 'heals the brokenhearted and binds up their wounds'?" (Ps. 147:3).

Yes, of course, I know that. But I just desperately need to be reminded. Thank you, my friend.

Loneliness is a part of being human. I often think of how lonely Jesus must have been during his tenure here with us on Earth. Surely, he desperately missed his Father. He became close to friends during his human thirty-three years, and sometimes they became sick and died. Lazarus, for instance. Jesus cried with Mary of Bethany when his beloved friend, Lazarus, died. How easy it is to forget that Jesus, himself, knew loneliness and sadness. Surely his heart broke when the rich young man turned his back to Jesus, unwilling to gain eternal life at the expense of his possessions. "Son," he might have thought, "You have no idea what I'm offering you, and what you're giving up." (see Mark 10:17-23). Think of how Jesus must have felt when he learned that Herod had beheaded Jesus' cousin, John. Heart-broken—for John, for John's mother, Elizabeth, for his father, Zachariah, and for himself. (see Mark 6:14-29). Or when his three friends, Peter, James, and John, fell asleep when Jesus asked them to pray in earnest for him (see Mark 14: 32-42). How disappointed Jesus must have been when one of his own, Peter, denied him (see Mark 14: 66-72); and when Judas betrayed him and helped bring about his death (see Luke 22:1-6). Or when only one healed leper, out of ten healed lepers, came back to Jesus to say a simple "thank you" (see Luke 17:11-19). You see, loneliness, sadness, and disappointment come to all human beings. And we, as Christian women, are given numerous opportunities every hour of every day to reach out and tell the brokenhearted that the Lord "heals the brokenhearted and binds up their wounds."

As I walked back to my room from the beach, I thought about Mary. It seemed that with every cresting wave on the sandy shore, I heard God's promise, again and again. "Come to me ... Come to me, all you who are weary and burdened, and I will give you rest" (Matt. 11:28). And all the way home, I prayed that Mary could hear it, too.

LONELINESS

Loneliness among women is an area of ministry where you and I desperately need to reach out. Lonely women surround us, yearning for someone to care. We can expect women who don't know Christ as Savior and Lord to be lonely. But why do Christian women become lonely? I believe that when God's own daughters become lonely, they have forgotten how much their Father loves them. Sometimes they just need a spiritual sister to remind them of the Father's love.

No doubt, you know a woman who is suffering from loneliness. It is a painful condition. Some women just seem more prone to loneliness than others. Women can feel lonely without good reason. Loneliness can be caused by many factors. Often our most lonely times come when a loved one dies, when we must depart from precious friends, or when we have endured a cross-country/cross-world move. A woman's heart can be wounded by loss and loneliness. Women who have lost a spouse, child, or close friend may keenly feel loneliness and loss.

With each fresh sting of loneliness, we can discover anew that the Lord is the healer of broken hearts. God suffers with us when we hurt. The Holy Spirit softly whispers to our hearts the lessons of faith we need to learn, and he does so gently and with great love. Perhaps loneliness is the very language of prayer. The Lord hears our lonely cries, binds up our wounds, and promises us a lifetime of tender healing care.

As I write these words, I think about a dear friend of mine. I'll call her Valerie. Beautiful, smart, a "mover and shaker," I loved spending time with her. Over the years, however, Valerie began to change in her personality. In little ways. She sometimes forgot where her friends lived when she drove to visit them. She forgot her grandchildren's names when she showed me their photographs. She'd forget a long-planned luncheon. I knew the signs and it broke my heart. I had seen the early symptoms of Alzheimer's in other friends. I also saw the outcome, how Alzheimer's took away their memory and mind. My friend Valerie and I shared so many wonderful memories—memories I knew, in a short time, she would no longer remember. After several years, what I had expected in Valerie's life came true. She became "another person," a person far from the Valerie I once knew.

Scripture convinces me that God does not *cause* Alzheimer's Disease. But, if it happens, then he must, for some reason, *allow* it. Why, I do not know. I don't even *pretend* to know. But I've learned that we must *trust* God in whatever happens. We must trust him, and just leave it there with him. And, when God gives us the opportunity to reach out in love to a hurting woman, we must be ready to comfort and help her. We must remind her that God is love, and that God loves her in her loneliness and pain.

SEEKING GOD WHEN WE'RE LONELY

When I come to "the lonely places" in my own life, I've discovered what author Myron Augsburger discovered. He writes: "Paradoxical as it may seem, the true cure for loneliness is to get alone with God, to allow one's self to rest in him. Loneliness," he writes, "is corrected by a sense of belonging to God."[1]

I have discovered that intimate fellowship with God is the only real cure for a lonely heart. Perhaps "loneliness is God's way of letting us know that it is time to reach out [to him]."[2]

It's so easy to wander away from God. We don't mean to; we just get tangled up with everyday life and its disappointments and demands. The pain of fresh loneliness can bring us back quickly into the waiting arms of God.

---

1   Myron S. Augsburger, *When Reason Fails* (Wheaton: Tyndale House Publishers, Inc., 1968), p. 75.

2   Billy Graham, "Are You Lonely?" *Decision* (June 1988), p. 3.

As we escape to the Lord, the quiet of loneliness can become a prayer in itself. Loneliness becomes solitude and solitude becomes prayer.

Years ago, feeling overwhelmed, frustrated, and weary with the busyness of life, and feeling very much alone in it all, I decided to start spending more time alone with the Lord. In fact, I decided to organize my whole day around my prayer and fellowship time with God.

The new schedule worked well. I rose very early in the mornings, sometimes as early as 4:00 a.m., I headed for a quiet mountain near my home so that I could pray and read Scripture—and be alone with God. I drove to the top of the small mountain, parked my car, and had quiet time with the Lord. I gazed at the stars and thanked my Creator. Sometimes I stared in silence and awe at the magnificent sunrise.

The morning soon became my favorite time of the whole day. I found I wanted to give God my best hours, my most awake and creative hours. For me, that time was early morning. During the day, I found too many interruptions. In the evenings, I was too tired to listen, read, and concentrate. There was something exciting, mysterious, and awesome about the early morning when all was dark and quiet, and the world around me slept.

I felt a special oneness with Christ as I sat in my warm car in the chill and dampness of the early morning, high on a mountaintop awaiting sunrise, and read in the Scriptures of the many times Jesus rose early and went into the mountains to pray. I looked forward to our early morning conversation.

I discovered once again that God created us to commune with Him, to love Him, to know Him. Only in our fellowship with God do we find and know great joy and peace. Even when life dumps its bills, disappointments, frustrations, and demands on us, we can live with God's joy filling our hearts.

I used to think of spending time alone with God as an opportunity to refuel so that I could better get on with life. Now I know that prayer and intimate communion with our Maker is not a pit stop to refresh and refuel. Prayer, communion, and fellowship with God is life itself, the reason for our existence. We were created to glorify God and to enjoy him forever. Sure, we have our responsibilities and our deadlines. While most of what we do is important and must be done, may we never lose sight of why we were created. May we tell hurting women everywhere of our chief purpose in life—to glorify God and enjoy him forever.

WHEN WE MEET OUR MARYS ...

Mary keenly felt the sting of loss—the death of her husband—even after ten years. Surely, each new loss we face brings its own painful kind of loneliness. But we must remind the world's hurting "Marys" that we don't face the loss alone. We can turn to the One who tells us, "I am the bread of life. He who comes to me will never go hungry, and he who believes in me will never be thirsty" (John 6:35).

We can share intimate moments with the Savior. He waits for us to come to him. He waits for us to come back to him whenever we drift away. Once we truly discover him, nothing else, no one else, can ever be as important to us.

"What we need first and foremost are intimate moments with the Savior…time spent all alone with Him, watching His model, listening to His counsel, feeling His touch. We need some way to connect our temporal world with His eternal perspective."[3]

St. Augustine said it so beautifully: "For Thou hast made us for Thyself, and our heart can find no rest until it rests in Thee."

Indeed, our hearts will be lonely until they find rest again in close intimate fellowship with our Lord Jesus Christ.

INTERCESSORY PRAYER

Above and beyond any other way you and I can reach out to hurting women today, we can reach out to them with prayer. When we pray for them, we tell them we dearly love them, that we care, that we share their struggle. We speak their language. We understand. When we pray for them, we bow before God on their behalf. When we pray for them, Jesus joins us in our prayers for them. We will see a miracle happen in their lives. Jesus can reach out to them with the close comfort of his friendship, and with eternal prayers that will forever bring them peace and joy. Such is the power within our grasp as you and I reach out with prayer to those women who suffer.

Jesus can bring them new life. "Come out!" Jesus calls to them and to us, as he called out to Lazarus

---

3   (In the foreword by Chuck Swindoll) Ken Gire, *Intimate Moments with the Savior* (Grand Rapids: Zondervan Publishing House, 1989), p. XI.

so long ago. And we leave our tombs of despair and hopelessness—our painful loneliness—and we step forward with new life, with new purpose in Christ.

4

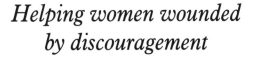

with compassion

*Helping women wounded
by discouragement*

| Bible Study: Read Luke 13:10-13 |

Only Luke's gospel mentions the woman who had spent eighteen years staring at the floor, unable to stand up, sit down, or straighten her crooked back.

Jesus and his disciples traveled through her city on their way from Galilee to Judea. On the Sabbath, as was his custom, Jesus entered the synagogue. She, too, entered the synagogue, and must have had to ignore pointing fingers and curious eyes. When Jesus saw her, he felt deep compassion. He reached out and touched her. Jesus healed her, even though healing on the Sabbath was against Mosaic law. When the ruler of the synagogue rebuked Jesus, he firmly exposed the inconsistency of those who would lead an ox to water on the Sabbath, yet who opposed the healing of this woman.

That Sabbath, Jesus also did something that made the religious leaders cringe. He referred to the woman as "a daughter of Abraham" (v. 16), a description reserved for the prestigious "sons" of Abraham. Before the upright religious folk, Jesus gave her a high place of honor when he affirmed that she, too, belonged to the family of Abraham.

Compassion. Deep compassion.

Recently, on a trip to Rome, I saw a "bent over" woman on the streets near the Roman Forum. She reminded me of the woman in this story. Things haven't changed much in that part of the world. I felt for that woman deep compassion, reached out to her, and helped her in a small way—with money. How I wish that I, too, could have "touched" her and healed her deformity.

We want to warn Jesus when he opposes the religious folk with this healing on the Sabbath: "Jesus, you will pay dearly for your many acts of compassion. You will soon be nailed to a cross by the very ones who cringe at your actions in the synagogue. But a cross can't stop your compassion. For you will also reach out with forgiving compassion to those who will drive the nails through your hands and feet, to those who will scourge your chest and back, to those who will spit at you and mock you while you breathe your final breath."

Jesus knew the risk. But he felt compassion was worth the price he would pay.

The story in Luke ended well. Something wonderful happened to the woman when Jesus touched her compassionately. Something totally unexpected. For the first time in eighteen years, she straightened her bent-over back, and stretched to her full height. (I hope she was eight feet tall!) We can imagine that while the "sons" of Abraham hung their heads in shame, she held her head high. And from that day on, we can imagine that this daughter of Abraham never missed another sunrise, sunset, or star-studded sky.

After eighteen years of staring at the ground, the woman surely must have felt defeated by life and lost hope of ever becoming whole again. But then Jesus came. His compassion restored health to her body and hope to her heart.

THE GREATEST ENEMY

We live in a world where many Christian women have lost hope. We meet and touch them every day.

Brokenness meets us on all sides: marriage, homes, relationships, dreams. For many women, life seems a continual cycle of brokenness and loss. They lose their loved ones, their vocations, their ambitions, and their youth. The cycle of loss is a part of everyday living and often leads to despair, the greatest enemy of the believer's heart.

Many women around us are encumbered with guilt and disturbed by painful pasts. Many are hurt by sickness, crushed by loss and failure, and wearied from seemingly fruitless waiting.

Many women are discouraged and confused; many have lost their jubilation. Life moves forward so quickly we seldom have adequate time to contemplate and reflect. In the race of life, we give our hurting hearts little time, little reflection for healing and insightful understanding. Running from one activity to another, Christian women can easily lose perspective, and forget that we race toward a finish line, the home that awaits us as believers in Christ. If we aren't alert, our hearts—the home of the Holy Spirit—can lose the laughter and joy of belonging to the family of God.

Several years ago I read a sad story of a man in Boston who had lost the one he loved. He found an unlocked parked car near a train station, and on the front seat, he left a $15,000 diamond engagement ring and a note that said: "Merry Christmas. Thank you for leaving your car door unlocked. Instead of stealing your car I gave you a present. Hopefully this will land in the hands of someone you love, for my love is gone now. Merry Christmas to you." We instinctively ache for that brokenhearted man, and wish we could reach out to him in his sadness. I often wonder what happened to the anonymous man.[1]

THE WHITE-GABLED HOUSE

Whenever I see the white-gabled house on a road near my home, I am reminded of how easily life's crises and problems can smother the gladness and delight of our hearts as they rest in God.

Day after day, workmen built the great Victorian style house. The magnificent house sat on a lovely spot surrounded by large green yards and mature trees. When the house was finished,

---

1   Found at: http://www.cnn.com/2005/US/12/15/ring.found.reuters. reut/index.html. Accessed: 12/16/05.

the construction crew packed their gear, and the builder put up a sign in the front lawn: "For Sale." Not long after, a large family with happy, playing children moved in. Soon pink begonia bloomed in the side gardens, tricycles and toys covered the stone walk, a pair of rocking chairs graced the front porch, and a new tire swing draped an old oak tree.

In the evenings, the soft lights within made the house seem to glow. I could imagine a contented growing family sharing a quiet evening together around the fireplace.

The house was no longer empty. It had come alive with the laughter and joy of family togetherness. The house sheltered a family. The house had become a home.

But then something happened. One day a construction crew pulled up beside the house and started work on a massive electrical facility. Several months later, the completed gray complex cast its ugly shadows across the white-gabled house.

Soon the lights inside were off and the house was empty. Gone were the tricycles and toys from the walk, the rocking chairs, and tire swing. The pink begonia wilted from lack of care. Taped onto the tall front Victorian window hung a red-lettered sign: "For Sale. Property of Central Bank."

It was a sad sight, as if the house had somehow died. The life inside had vanished. It seemed a hollow shell where laughter, joy, and family once lived.

What happened to the house is not unlike what can happen to Christian women today. We are all like the empty house until we give our hearts and lives to God through Jesus Christ. God, the Holy Spirit, moves into our "house" and we take on signs of new life. God brings to our home laughter, joy, and familial fellowship with him. We seem to glow with the light of the One who illumines our lives and enriches them with eternal meaning. We enjoy quiet evenings in rich fellowship with him. Jesus Christ becomes our lives, and we begin to grow in our exciting newfound faith.

Who knows what kind of shadow can fall across the Christian woman's path and cause her to lose her laughter, visible joy, and fellowship with Christ. Perhaps a tragedy, loss, or heartbreak can cause her to despair. In her desperation, she sometimes gives up on life. When she does, it is as if something within her has died. Her inner light no longer shines brightly. The rich, full fellowship she once shared now seems empty.

I saw this happen recently with a friend of mine. First, her grown son suffered a heart attack and literally "dropped dead." His unexpected and untimely death broke her heart and spirit. Then, not long after, her husband died from a disease. She became very sad and lonely and pulled away from her friends for a long time. My friend knew, however, that just because she had experienced two tragedies and felt sad and in great grief that God hadn't forgotten her. As a believer, she didn't lose her place in God's family. She was his daughter, saved by Christ. She knew she would always be his daughter because that is God's promise to her and to all those who believe and accept his gift of grace and life.

"God began doing a good work in you," Paul wrote. "And he will continue it until it is finished when Jesus Christ comes again" (Phil. 1:6 NCV).

A "shadow" fell over her life when she lost the two people she most loved. And for a long time, my friend lost her visible joy. She felt despair, and loss of hope in her sadness.

It's not a new problem among Christians. The apostle Paul saw it happen, too. He saw the despair among the early believers who were harshly persecuted by the Roman government for following Christ. Many quickly lost heart and gave up. Paul wrote lengthy, loving letters to encourage them, and to tell them not to lose heart even when they were beaten down. He told them to remember Jesus Christ and to look to the hope and glory that awaited them (see 2 Cor. 4:17).

Sometimes it seems, in our greatest sadness, that God has deserted us, that He seems nowhere around us, that our prayers seem to no longer reach Him. With our hearts in turmoil, we search for rest and peace, and cannot seem to find it.

But God is there. He is with you when your heart is broken. As His daughter, you are never alone. He is never far from you. Sometimes it's just hard to see him in the dark storms of life.

This is the message we must tell our broken-hearted spiritual sisters when they face hardships, when they feel alone and lonely. And this is the message they must tell us when we, too, experience life's unexpected crises. Sisters reach out and help one another in their greatest time of need. They remind each other that the Father loves them dearly, and stays closer to them than their own breathing.

I KNOW FIRSTHAND ABOUT BROKEN HEARTS...

I remember the early Saturday morning my beloved grandmother, "Mama," died. It was a turning point in my life. Mama and I were so close. We loved each other as much as a granddaughter and grandmother could ever love. From my birth, Mama tucked me into the high, quilt-covered bed and told me stories about Jesus and his love for me. She and my grandfather nurtured me in the Christian faith. How I loved them and appreciated them for their faithful devotion to me!

Whenever I relive that early Saturday morning, the old yellow porch swing comes to mind. Before Mama's death, I would sit in the swing for hours, look out beyond the trees and small flower garden, and contemplate God's goodness, his love for me, and my gratefulness to him. The swing proved a happy place for me; it was the secret spot where God and I often met.

But all that changed the Saturday morning my grandmother died. Since I was only ten days away from giving birth to my daughter, her namesake, I couldn't attend the funeral 300 miles away. My doctor told me the long trip would be too uncomfortable and too risky at this stage of my pregnancy.

All that day, I sat in the porch swing and cried. In fact, I cried all the next week. The laughter, joy, and fellowship that had become symbolic of the porch swing had disappeared. Instead, I shouted angry questions at God. "Why, God, did you let Mama die before my daughter was born? Why couldn't you let Mama live just ten more days to see her precious new great-granddaughter?"

Mama had so looked forward to my daughter, Alyce's birth. She had hoped to live long enough to cuddle her tiny namesake in her arms as she had once held and cuddled me and my firstborn son. I couldn't understand why God allowed what seemed to me such cruel timing.

Ten days later, still sad and brokenhearted, I went into Caesarean surgery. At one point in the surgical preparations, my crying overwhelmed me. My doctor stopped and asked me if I felt physical pain. I shook my head. "No," I wanted to tell him, "physical pain couldn't hurt half as much as this pain in my heart."

I felt no particular closeness to God the week between Mama's death and my surgery. Little did I know that even when I thought God was far away from me, he was still at work, loving, healing, and restoring my broken heart.

I was soon to discover God's love for me anew. Late that Tuesday morning, when I returned to my room from surgery, the nurse placed into my tired arms a beautiful healthy newborn daughter. My very own Alyce—a gift from God.

New life pierced the gloom in my heart. New life cut through the devastating shroud of death that had surrounded me and swallowed me. God blessed me with a new Alyce, not one to take Mama's place, but one to carry on her name and memory. I knew that whenever I looked at my daughter's face or called her name, I would think of my grandmother.

Immediately, my heart overflowed with tenderness, joy, and thankfulness. I breathed a heartfelt prayer of renewed fellowship with God. Once again, as I lay still in that hospital bed nursing my newborn daughter, I felt God close to me.

I know, from that experience, and others, that the heart can begin again. Even when we are engulfed by troubles and don't know what to do, even when the pain inside is more than we can stand, God doesn't leave us. He stays beside us, working all things toward our good and the good of his kingdom. God is always as close as a prayer. Through all our painful ordeals, God never stops whispering his words of love, encouragement, and hope to our weary hearts. "We know that in all things God works for the good of those who love him, who have been called according to his purpose" (Rom. 8:28). That is God's promise to you and me.

How often God can use our brokenness! When, as a teenager, I fell off a pony (he was standing still) and broke my left arm, my doctor set it in a cast and promised me: "Denise, when your bone heals, it'll be stronger than it was before you broke it."

Pastor Rick Warren wants to hire only people in his church that have been broken! He writes: "I've told my staff many times we don't want to hire anyone who hasn't had problems in life. They're usually not very effective in ministry. I want people who have been broken. It makes people more real; it makes them more honest."[2]

---

2   Found at: http://www.pastors.com/blogs/ministrytoolbox/archive/2010/
01/27/a-holy-god-a-surrendered-life-a-fearful-thing.asp Accessed: 1/28/10.

OUR TRIUMPH

No doubt, when Jesus' closest friends climbed to the mountaintops with him, listened to him tell wonderful stories about God's kingdom, and sat around the fire talking long into the night, they could not have imagined what the future would bring. They knew Jesus personally and shared with him a rare friendship.

Then that ominous Friday came, and in their unexpected terror they scattered. They watched their beloved friend slapped, spit upon, abused, and finally executed by Roman soldiers. All their dreams for the future seemed shattered. Their hearts broken, they lost hope and hid.

They spent a sad Saturday morning enveloped by the darkness of death, crying for their dear friend, and wondering why God allowed this terrible tragedy.

Surely, the disciples and friends of Jesus thought that dark Saturday would last forever. Never had they felt so sorrowful. They had lost their hope. Jesus, their Lord and friend, was dead and buried.

But God had other plans. The next morning, when Mary Magdalene walked to Jesus' grave in the predawn hours, she didn't find a dead Jesus there. Instead she heard Jesus call her name! Sunday had dawned bright with the resurrected Christ. Mary's sad heart filled with hope and became jubilant again. She ran to the disciples to share the good news. "I have seen the Lord!" she proclaimed.

Did the mourning, weeping disciples believe Mary? No! "When they heard that Jesus was alive and that [Mary] had seen him, they did not believe it"

(Mark 16:11). Only when Jesus appeared personally to the disciples, pointed out his pierced hands and feet, ate with them, and then "opened their minds so they could understand the Scriptures" (Luke 24:45), did they finally believe Jesus had risen.

Once the disciples were convinced, resurrection filled their hearts. They were never again the same. For they, too, had seen the Lord.

True, we may have troubles all around us, but we are never defeated. We often don't know what to do, but we cannot give up. We are often persecuted, but God never leaves us.

We hurt sometimes, but we are never destroyed. God is always close to us in all our trying circumstances.

What do we do when our hearts are filled with heaviness, encumbered with guilt, disturbed by painful pasts? What do we do when we are wounded by sickness, crushed by loss and failure, and wearied from seemingly fruitless waiting? What do we do when our hearts are tired and confused and have lost their jubilation?

We trust. We continue to trust the One who has promised to stay close to us and to work our trouble for good. God, through his Son, Jesus Christ, reaches out to us and forgives, helps us to overcome sorrowful pasts, brings rest from our sickness, carries us through loss and failure, and gives us vision and hope in our waiting.

Tell your troubled spiritual sister that she can trust God! Tell her that her troubled and broken heart can become a heart at peace again. Tell her God can stir the cold ashes of a despondent life and make it glow anew with laughter and joy and renewed family fellowship. Won't you share this truth with a woman who needs to hear it? Surely that is what a sister's keeper is supposed to do.

5

REACHING

with affirmation

OUT

Helping victims of spouse abuse

| Bible Study: Read Luke 7:36-50 |

She was a woman who must have lost her sense of self. Mistreated by the people in her daily life, she undoubtedly carried a heavy heart and felt worthless. How urgently she must have needed a word of affirmation, a reason to be alive, a purpose, and a peace.

Scripture refers to her as a sinner—no name, just a "sinner." She probably was a prostitute who did business on the streets of Nain, a village of southwest Galilee. Prostitution was tolerated in those days, if the woman was unmarried.

Why did she work as a prostitute? Scripture doesn't tell us, but, in biblical times, divorce proved easy for a husband. Women often found themselves out on the street, with neither shelter nor bread. Divorced women (and widows) had few work options to keep food in their stomachs. They basically had two choices: to beg on the streets for a few coins from the compassionate, or to sell their bodies to men.

The religious Pharisees must have despised this woman—a "sinner." Can you just imagine how upset they were when she entered the home of Simon the Pharisee uninvited? Simon was hosting a men's dinner party for Jesus that evening. No self-respecting woman would burst into a room full of men.

But she did. She must have felt she had nothing to lose. She held an alabaster flask of perfume. Upon seeing Jesus, she dropped at his feet and began to cry. Her tears poured onto his feet, washing from them the dust and dirt of Galilee's streets. She then wiped his feet clean with her long hair and kissed them. She broke the flask of treasured fragrance and anointed his feet with tenderness and love.

By this time, Simon, the host, had seen enough. He scolded her with harsh, critical words. Simon even questioned Jesus' integrity for allowing such a woman to touch him.

But Jesus could see through her tarnished reputation. He could see the woman's heart, a heart that sought forgiveness and purpose in life. Her heart cried out for a kind word.

The Pharisees must have felt horror and surprise when Jesus did not criticize the woman. He did not seem offended. He did not push her away. Instead, Jesus affirmed her in front of the room filled with narrow-sighted, self-righteous men.

"Do you see this woman?" Jesus asked Simon. "I came into your house. You did not give me any water for my feet, but she wet my feet with her tears and wiped them with her hair" (v. 44).

Jesus continued: "You did not give me a kiss, but this woman, from the time I entered, has not stopped kissing my feet. You did not put oil on my head, but she has poured perfume on my feet" (vv. 45-46). Without apology, Simon had neglected these elementary and expected gestures of Middle Eastern hospitality.

Then Jesus astounded them all, and, no doubt, left the men speechless. "Therefore I tell you, her many sins have been forgiven—for she loved much" (v. 47).

A sudden hush must have swept the room. Can you imagine the men's reactions, too shocked to speak?

In the moment of quiet, Jesus turned to the woman who still knelt by his feet. Perhaps he smiled at her. Perhaps Jesus took her hand in his and brought her up to her feet so that she could stand before him and look directly into his eyes.

"Your sins are forgiven," he told her. "Your faith has saved you." Then Jesus spoke three more words that would no doubt remain within her heart and memory for the rest of her life: "Go in peace" (vv. 48, 50). Jesus forgave her and affirmed her. On the streets of Galilee, she no longer would be referred to as the "sinner." Jesus had restored her sense of self. She became known from that day as the "woman who loved much," the woman Jesus honored.

The nameless woman who entered Simon's house in pain departed in peace. Not only did Jesus publicly forgive her, but he publicly affirmed her. The woman who bowed down, cleaned, kissed, and anointed Jesus' street-dirty feet departed that day with a freshly cleansed heart and a brand-new life.

It's interesting that perfume—an expensive luxury—has been around for the past 4,000 years! Sometimes the beautifully-designed perfume containers were more costly than the perfume itself. Ancients often burned perfume (incense) in religious ceremonies. In biblical times, people buried their dead loved ones with perfume. Remember that the wise men brought baby Jesus perfume—frankincense and myrrh. We do not know where the woman got the perfume, nor the cost. It might have been a gift, possibly the only thing of worth she owned. Did she have some insight into the upcoming death of Jesus, and she wanted to anoint his body with perfume? Perhaps. Scripture doesn't tell us. Perhaps God had given her spiritual insight, and with her alabaster bottle of perfume, led her to "announce" the death of Jesus. Maybe it was all she owned, and she wanted to give everything she had to the Lord.

How interesting that Jesus asked the question of the men in the room: "Do you see this woman?" Of course they saw her! She crashed their party. They all focused eyes of hatred and disgust on her. Perhaps Jesus spoke of "seeing" deeper than outward appearances. Maybe he was referring to her heart—a broken heart, a contrite heart.

Jesus might ask the same question of us as we go about our daily busy lives. "Do you 'see' this hurting woman standing beside you in the grocery store line?

Or sitting beside you in the church pew? Do you really 'see' her—do you 'see' her heart?" She may be the woman driving the car next to yours, or the young mother sitting on the edge of the community swimming pool with her young child. She may be your mother, grandmother, daughter, or granddaughter. She may be the neighbor down the street.

I believe Jesus wants us to look closely at the women beside us. Are they hurting? Are they women who are mistreated by the people in their daily life? Does she carry a heavy heart and feel worthless, useless? How can you and I reach out to her with love and affirmation, the same way Jesus reached out to the "sinful" woman who crashed Simon's party?

MARGARET'S STORY

Let me tell you about Margaret. She was a lovely Christian woman with silver-streaked hair, a petite figure, and a gentle, warm smile. She had a certain sophistication about her, a natural charm. Yet beneath her appearance, she was a woman who had endured a life no one deserves.

Margaret had finished college and married. Together she and her new husband set up a home, had a son, and looked forward to a storybook marriage.

Within a few years, however, for no apparent or predictable reason, Margaret's husband began to abuse her. Physically. Emotionally. Verbally. Sexually. What began as a once in a while slap became routine, life-threatening beatings, beatings that left her scarred outside and inside, beatings that destroyed her self-esteem.

With little support from her family, Margaret endured the beatings for as long as she could. She tried hard to be a loving wife and a good Christian mother. She tried desperately to hold her deteriorating marriage together and hide her terrible secret. She kept trying to change so that her husband might love her and be kind to her. He had convinced her that his rage and his abuse was her fault.

But Margaret could not keep her marriage together. The beating proved too brutal. She feared for her life and for the life of her young son. Her heart broken, her dreams shattered, Margaret's marriage ended in divorce.

THE PROBLEM OF DOMESTIC VIOLENCE

Margaret's story is a common one. Look at the women around you. Many homes today are not what God intended. Instead of a place where love and acceptance are the norm, violence and abuse are everyday experiences. I am no longer shocked when I hear about spouse abuse in Christian homes.

In researching my book *What Women Wish Pastors Knew* (Zondervan, 2008), I asked women in the United States and several European countries to answer the question: "What do you want your pastor to know about you, your family, etc?" Hundreds of women filled out the surveys and returned them to me. Time after time, I read their accounts of spouse abuse. "Please," they said, "Tell the world's pastors that women are hurting, and they are *being hurt* in their own homes by their husbands!"

When Zondervan released the new book, the survey answers astounded most of the pastors I spoke to.

They couldn't believe that so many Christian women, married to Christian husbands, endured some form of spouse abuse!

Domestic abuse knows no boundaries. Educational background, income, class, race, or faith seem to make little difference. Our society was shocked by the discovered beatings of Nicole Simpson by her husband. Most of America stayed glued to their televisions during the O. J. Simpson murder trial. Many women are suffering in secret and in silence around the world.

Spouse abuse is nothing new. It's as old as time itself. Our present society has long known about spouse abuse, but fear, embarrassment, and practical concerns covered it with a blanket of silence. Today we are becoming increasingly aware of the unbelievable frequency and seriousness of spouse abuse.

Over the past two decades, violence by an intimate partner has become identified throughout the world as a serious physical and mental health concern. *Spouse abuse*, in particular, was recognized at the Fourth World Conference on Women held in Beijing in 1995 as a human rights concern worldwide.

Early definitions of spouse abuse referred only to the physical injury a husband perpetrated against his wife. More recent research broadened this definition to include sexual abuse, marital rape, emotional or psychological abuse, and coercion. The United Nations' Commission on the Status of Women presently defines domestic violence as "any act of gender based violence that results in physical, sexual or psychological harm or suffering to women, including threats of such acts, coercion, or arbitrary deprivation of liberty whether occurring in public or private life."[1]

Studies show that between one quarter and one half of all women in the world have been abused by intimate partners. Worldwide, 40-70 per cent of all female murder victims are killed by an intimate partner.[2]

Another study reveals that in the U.S., every nine seconds a woman is physically abused by her husband. Within the last year, 7 per cent of American women (3.9 million) who are married, or living with someone, were physically abused, and 37 per cent (20.7 million) were verbally or emotionally abused by their spouse or partner.[3]

ONE OF THE BEST-KEPT SECRETS

Spouse abuse is as intense a problem in the body of Christ as it is outside the church. In other words, a Margaret may be sitting beside you on the church pew on any given Sunday morning in any country in the world. It's unbelievable and frightening. Violence appears to be growing even among churchgoing families.

What does spouse abuse include? Slaps, kicks, and other forms of physical battering; sexual assault; rape; and even murder. Causing emotional pain with destructive put-downs, threats, or name-calling also

---

1   Found at: http://family.jrank.org/pages/1630/Spouse-Abuse.html. Accessed: 1/27/10.

2   Found at: http://www.stopvaw.org/Prevalence_of_Domestic_Violence. html. Accessed: 1/27/10.

3   Found at: http://dso.uncc.edu/women/TBN_Web/stats.html. Accessed: 1/27/10.

is abuse. Abuse can be spousal neglect or "the silent knight syndrome"—consistently ignoring the spouse, or failing to communicate or bond in relationship.

The male batterer may come from a violent home. He often blames others for his problems or denies he has a problem. He may use drinking and wife-beating to cope with stress.

The abused wife often tries to keep peace in the family at all costs. She is overly trusting of others, and assumes the guilt for her husband's abusive behavior. She feels helpless and hopeless to stop the violence, and as a result often suffers from feelings of worthlessness.

MARGARET'S LIFE AFTER DIVORCE

After Margaret's divorce, she and her son were left financially hurting, a common occurrence among today's newly divorced women in the world. Society calls them "the new poor." As a single mother with few financial resources and memories of the humiliating experience of battering, Margaret suffered from low self-esteem and a severe lack of confidence. She feared a future that looked sad, scary, and hopeless.

Then Margaret met her "prince." Stephen, a widower, was tall, attractive, financially stable, and a skilled surgeon. Stephen offered her a strong shoulder to cry on, a deep respect for her personhood, and a sympathetic ear that listened with patience.

Everyone liked Stephen. He was a kind, caring, gentle man. He held an important leadership role in his church. Stephen was esteemed by many devoted patients. He was almost too good to be true.

Within nine months after her divorce, Stephen offered Margaret a beautiful life and a hope-filled future as his wife. Margaret was thrilled. It seemed like a dream come true. Margaret would no longer journey through life alone but with a kind Christian man who would love her, affirm her, and help her find her lost sense of self. She began to feel hope and renewal within her tired heart.

For the first two weeks, Margaret lived a blissful life as Stephen's wife, growing from the nourishment he gave her, basking in the sunshine of his love for her. But then her happily-ever-after storybook marriage became a living nightmare.

Margaret remembers: "As I was changing our bed, I dropped the dirty sheets on the floor—not the clean sheets, the dirty sheets! For no apparent reason, Stephen became enraged. I was shocked! That's the day I discovered Stephen's violent temper."

The battering began. Margaret's sense of hope and happiness was smothered by bewilderment and despair. Stephen began by hitting Margaret, and the violence intensified. He would throw her against furniture, grab her hair, and shove her to the floor. Stephen used the same violent attacks on Margaret that she had, in confidence, told him her first husband used to hurt her.

Neighbors could hear Margaret's screams during the frequent beatings, and sometimes gathered on the street beneath the bedroom window. "They knew what was going on," Margaret said, "but no one knew what to do. And no one wanted to get involved."

Stephen was liked and respected in the church where he had been a lifetime member. In spite of routine beatings, Margaret devoted herself to Stephen and to his church. She told no one in the church about the abuse. And no one at church seemed to suspect it.

"Stephen was careful to bruise only the parts of my body and legs that my clothes would hide," Margaret said.

After a beating to the head, Margaret suffered permanent hearing loss in one ear. Her doctor wrote "trauma-caused" on her chart.

Margaret also endured severe emotional abuse. Stephen called her names, tapped the home phone, and allowed her little contact with family and friends.

Margaret stayed married to Stephen and endured his abuse for fifteen years. "People often ask me why I didn't leave him, why I stayed with him so long," Margaret said. "During those years, I felt so alone, alienated, and worthless. I lost the will to live. I was so under Stephen's control, I couldn't even think for myself. I felt as though I didn't belong to the human race."

Margaret tried several times to kill herself but each time she failed. She later found out that Stephen had also battered his first wife, Sandra. After twenty years of daily abuse, Sandra committed suicide.

Several years into the marriage, Stephen became even more hostile. "I was so terrified of him, I moved into the guest bedroom and had a deadbolt lock put on my door," Margaret said. "I really believed my life was in danger."

SHATTERED DREAMS
Perhaps you know someone who is hiding the terrible secret of spouse abuse. She lives from day to day in

fear, confusion, and despair. Beating after beating, she is being destroyed. As a girl she dreamed of a happy marriage with the man she loved. She wanted everything a home represents: love, trust, honesty, companionship, compassion, faithfulness, strong loving arms to embrace her, a secure shelter from the world, and a warm nest in which to rear her children. But the pain of battering has left her dream in shambles. She feels unsafe and unloved in her own home, and she is ready to give up. She doesn't know what to do. She keeps hoping the abuse will stop and things at home will get better. But after so many promises, after so much pain, she quickly is losing heart and hope.

The walls of many homes around the world hide hurting women who are terrified of their husbands and afraid for their children. They are women who have lost heart, who have lost the will to live. They are the women who sit around you and me in church on Sunday mornings living lives of physical and emotional abuse. They wear long-sleeved blouses in hot weather to cover their bruises and cuts. They secretly cry for help.

You and I need to reach out to these hurting women. As sisters in Christ, as members of his body, we all share the problem of battering. When one member hurts, other members hurt as well. When one member is wounded, we all cringe in pain. We cannot function properly as a Christian body when even one of us is being crippled by another's violent hand.

How can you and I reach out to abused women? We can reach out in several ways. First, we need to help her remove herself and her children from the hostile environment. We can recommend good Christian attorneys and counselors, people who know what to do and how to do it. We can become aware of shelters in our communities and volunteer to work at local domestic abuse centers. We can also contribute to the financial support of victims.

Second, we need to let the abused woman know that someone cares for her, that she is created by God as a person of infinite worth. She does not need to be pitied, but empowered to become all that God intended her to be. Your support as a friend and as a church can do much to help her regain her feeling of worth. In that way, you and I can reach out to her in the same way Jesus reached out—with affirmation.

It's not easy to reach out to a woman who desperately hides the secret of spouse abuse. We often feel it's none of our business, and it's uncomfortable to approach another in pain. Sometimes if our suspicions aren't confirmed, we become embarrassed. But we must reach out. The wounded woman needs God's heart and God's hands—her spiritual sister—to bring her back to her feet, to look at life with hope and self-confidence. Without intervention, the abuse will not stop. It most cases, the abuse will accelerate.

A HOPELESS FUTURE?

Margaret was the victim of two violent, abusive marriages. For many years, she believed the future held no hope for her. But Margaret's turning point came. Margaret finally found hope.

After an unusually tense confrontation with Stephen, fearing for her life, Margaret worked up the courage to call an attorney friend. With the attorney's help, Margaret was able to leave the abusive home. She also stopped going to Stephen's church. Soon, a friend reached out and invited Margaret to her church. The members were kind and welcomed her with open arms. Margaret felt at home.

"That's what I needed most," Margaret remembers, "a friend who affirmed me, who reached out to me with understanding. I will be eternally grateful to her."

During the last three years at the church, Margaret has found the support, encouragement, and emotional healing she so desperately needed. Her self-esteem is growing. When she thought no one cared, Christian women reached out to her.

"My Sunday School class members call me and make me feel like a part of the church. They listen to me and make me feel that someone really cares. When I had minor surgery, my pastor and some members greeted me at the hospital. I feel surrounded by the church's love and prayers. It's like a brand-new life."

THE HAUNTING QUESTION

Within the noise and chaos of everyday life, within the echo of criticism and harsh words, within the pain and terror that many women suffer today, Jesus stops, looks at you and me, and asks: "Do you *see* this woman?"

6

with needed help

*Helping victims of childhood
sexual abuse*

| Bible Study: Read Mark 5:21-34 |

We don't know her name. We know only that she was
a woman with a dreadful secret, a secret that lived in
her heart and mind every day. For twelve years she
suffered with a humiliating condition in her society,
a hemorrhage that caused her to bleed continuously.
According to Mosaic law, the constant flow of blood
made her unclean. The law prohibited her from
touching or being touched. She spent everything she
had on doctors who could offer no cure.

How she must have craved the warm touch of
a friend's hand, a loving embrace, a husband's arms
around her. Yet she had to remain alone, alienated
from others and from life itself.

Devastated. Ashamed. Humiliated. That's how the hemorrhaging woman must have felt the day Jesus walked into her city. But wait. If she were here today, the story she would tell might be this:

"I had heard about Jesus. The townspeople said Jesus could heal sick people. 'Please let it be true, God,' I had prayed that morning to the God of Abraham. Jesus was talking with an important man in the city. Jairus, I believe. Someone had said Jairus was asking Jesus to make his little daughter well. They walked in haste toward Jairus's home. On the way, however, a great crowd gathered around the two men. I guess everyone was curious about the Healer. For a moment, the Healer and Jairus were hemmed in and unable to move.

"I had been standing on my feet for a long time. I could feel the blood pouring heavily from me. I worried that it might spill onto the ground. Then I saw my chance, my chance to reach out to Jesus, the Healer. 'If only…if only…' I whispered under my breath as I made my way through the crowd. 'Could this Jesus really heal me? Could he stop this awful, embarrassing flow of blood?'

"The law demanded I shout 'unclean, unclean' when I approached others. But there was no time. I was so anxious to touch Jesus, I slipped unannounced through the swarm of people.

"Trembling, I reached out and touched his clothes— just a tassel hanging from the hem. Immediately I felt the flow of blood stop. I felt the power of his healing rush through me. I was healed! After all the years of suffering…of isolation…of spending money on false cures…I was finally healed!

"I turned around to hurry home, escape the crowd, and thank the God of Abraham for this Healer—this Jesus.

"But then what I feared most happened. Jesus stopped. He looked around. Somehow he knew, he knew I had touched him.

"'Who touched my clothes?' (v. 30) he asked. I knew I would be punished for touching a man of God for, in my touching him, I had made him ceremonially unclean. I wondered what the punishment would be. I mustered up all my courage and stepped forward. Falling at his feet, I confessed to him the truth. Then I trembled as I awaited harsh words and certain reproof.

"To my surprise, his voice was gentle. 'Daughter,' he said to me. I looked up into his eyes. He called me 'daughter,' as if I actually belonged to him, to his family. It had been a long time since anyone had so lovingly, so purely, called me 'daughter.'

"He continued speaking to me. 'Your faith has healed you. Go in peace and be freed from your suffering' (v. 34).

"Then he was gone and the crowd disappeared with him. I stood there for a long time and pondered his words, remembered his eyes, and repeated aloud his blessing of peace.

"Devastation, shame, humiliation. All of these were gone from my life. I trusted Jesus with my painful secret. I reached out to him, and he reached back to me with the love, help, and healing I needed most."

A HUMILIATING SECRET

We don't know her name. She is yet another anonymous woman in the Bible. We only know that she was a woman with a dreadful secret. For years she had suffered with it.

Likewise, a humiliating secret lives in our contemporary society, in our world. Devastated. Ashamed. Humiliated. That's how many women feel who have experienced childhood sexual abuse. The results are severely hurting women, women who are devastated and ashamed, women who desperately need healing help.

For many years, Liz carried a heavy load of unresolved anger, fear, and loneliness. She was troubled by frightening recurring nightmares. Liz described herself as "an open wound desperately wanting to be healed but festering with anger and hate." Her childhood was stolen by her father, a man who used and abused her selfishly, secretly for years and then abandoned her mother and family.

Liz was one of the fortunate ones, however. Liz reached out to a Christian counselor. Healing didn't happen overnight; but with the counselor's help, Liz has been able to put the terrible ordeal behind her and move forward with her life.

CHILDHOOD SEXUAL ABUSE

Sexual abuse is unlike any other childhood abuse. It is degrading, painful, and confusing to a child. It robs a child of a childhood—a time that should be carefree and creative and that, once lost, can never be recovered.

We see child sexual abuse around our entire planet. It happened in Sambava, Madagascar. A nine-year-old, Kenia, was savagely sexually-assaulted by her uncle. The attack left her in constant pain, incontinent, anorexic, and tore her colon. Doctors had to perform a colostomy on the child. Her attacker, after four years, still walks a free man. Among sub-Saharan Africa's children, this is a distressingly common story. Even as this region races to adopt many of the developed world's norms for children, from universal education to limits on child labor, child sexual abuse remains stubbornly difficult to eradicate. In much of the continent, child advocates say, perpetrators are shielded by the traditionally low status of girls, a view that sexual abuse should be dealt with privately, and justice systems that constitute obstacle courses for victims. Data is sparse, and sexual violence is notoriously underreported. But South African police reports give an inkling of the sweep of this child victimization. In the twelve months that ended in March 2005, the police estimated that there were about 23,000 cases of child rape. In contrast, England and Wales, with nine million more people than South Africa, reported 13,300 rapes of all females in the most recent 12-month period. The problem is by no means unique to Africa. While a survey of nine countries last year by the World Health Organization, found the highest incidence of child sexual abuse in Namibia (more than one in five women there reported having been sexually abused before the age of fifteen) the survey also found high rates of sexual abuse in Peru, Japan, and Brazil, among others.[1]

Child sexual abuse is a significant public health problem in the United States and across the world. In the United States, one out of every three females, and one out of every five males, have been victims of sexual abuse before the age of eighteen years. Sexual abuse occurs across all ethnic/racial, socioeconomic, and religious groups. Unfortunately, sexual abuse is considered a relatively common experience in the lives of many children.[2]

One report claims that child sexual abuse in India begins as early as five, ratchets up dramatically during pre-pubescence, and peaks at 12 to 16 years. Some 21 per cent of respondents acknowledged experiencing severe sexual abuse like rape, sodomy, fondling or exposure to pornographic material. Ironically, 71 per cent of sexual assault cases in India go unreported. India is home to more than 375 million children, comprising nearly 40 per cent of the country's population, the largest number of minors in any country in the world. India hosts the world's largest number of sexually abused children, at a far higher rate than any other country.[3]

---

1   Found at: http://www.nytimes.com/2006/12/01/world/africa/01iht-africa.3738426.html?_r=1. Accessed: 1/28/10.

2   Found at: http://www.childtrauma.org/ctamaterials/sexual_abuse.asp. Accessed: 1/28/10.

3   Found at: http://www.asiasentinel.com/index.php?option=com_content&task=view&id=476&Itemid=34. Accessed: 1/28/10.

Another study gives heart-breaking statistics:

1 out of 3 women worldwide has experienced rape or sexual assault.

In some countries, up to one-third of adolescent girls report forced sexual initiation.

Hundreds of thousands of women and girls throughout the world are forcibly trafficked and prostituted each year.

A report of seven different countries found that more than 60 per cent of sexual assault victims know their attackers.

A large number of sexual assault victims are less than fifteen years of age.

In South East Asia, 40 per cent of girls are being sold into prostitution to feed their families.[4]

An October, 2006, article in *Time* magazine reports that: "Two years ago, Cambodia was the number one destination for pedophiles …. Cambodia is still a destination for child abusers, but it has been surpassed in the last two years by even more lawless places such as the Dominican Republic, Bosnia, and Guatemala.[5]

Childhood sexual abuse usually leaves its young victim hurting and suffering with a deep sense of shame, guilt, and worthlessness. It can leave

---

4   Stats found at: http://www.gmu.edu/depts/unilife/sexual/brochures/WorldStats2005.pdf. Accessed: 1/28/10.

5   Found at:http://www.time.com/time/world/article/0,8599,1543174-3,00.html. Accessed: 1/28/10.

a lifelong scar. Those feelings are intensified when the producer of that shame and pain is the girl's father, the person who is supposed to love her, care for her, guide her spiritually, and be her strength throughout her journey to womanhood.

Only within the past few years have women begun to more freely share this humiliating secret. Childhood sexual abuse is a form of bullying, only worse. A little girl cannot understand this terrible trauma caused by an adult she trusts. She doesn't have the maturity to grasp what is happening to her. She is at the complete mercy of someone older, bigger, and smarter. An innocent little girl is no match for an adult abuser.

WHAT IS SEXUAL ABUSE?

Sexual abuse or molestation is defined as "any sexual touch by force, trickery, or bribery between two people where there is an imbalance of age, size, power, or knowledge. The power imbalance and intimidation results in the child living with a dreaded secret."[6] Sexual abuse happens in families of all social levels, regardless of income, community prominence, or church affiliation.

Meet Alice Huskey. Her father began sexually abusing her when she was only three years old. The abuse continued almost daily for the next decade.

Alice came forward with her story and reached out for treatment. She then wrote about her ordeal hoping to help others who are hiding the unresolved pain of childhood sexual abuse.

---

6   Virginia D. and Ratliff, Bill J. "Abused Children." in *When Children Suffer,* ed. Andrew D. Lester (Philadelphia, PA: The Westminster Press, 1987), p. 134.

Alice revealed that because of her father's angry threats on her life, she kept the dark secret inside, afraid someone would find out about it. At age thirteen, Alice finally decided to tell her unsuspecting mother about her father's demanding and intimidating behavior.

After telling her mother, however, Alice panicked.

"I had blurted out the secret myself!" she remembered. "There was nothing I could do now but bear the consequences. Mother reacted in shock, but managed to do the right thing. Most importantly, she believed me. And then she took action."[7]

Alice's mother confided in friends, asked their advice, and took her daughter to the sheriff's office. Not long afterward, two deputy sheriffs arrested her father. But the nightmare had only begun. The news broke quickly in her neighborhood and church community.

"It seemed as if some of my mother's friends at church were supportive," she admits, "but it was so painful to hear snatches of gossip at church and in the community. I remember going to the church picnic and wanting only to stay close to my mother. She was all I had and I needed her. I didn't want to leave her side because I was afraid. I felt as if I had a big sign around my neck saying 'dirty, ugly, naughty, guilty—stay away.'"[8]

The case came to trial. Alice described the experience in one word: "Devastating." Her father was acquitted with only a short stay in custody for observation. Her parents divorced, and Alice went

---

7   Alice Huskey, *Stolen Childhood: What You Need to Know about Sexual Abuse* (Downers Grove, IL: InterVarsity Press, 1990), p. 14.

8   Alice Huskey, Ibid.

to live with a foster mother. Her secret was out, and the shame, humiliation, and gossip followed her everywhere she went.

THE PROBLEM OF CHILD SEXUAL ABUSE

Believe it or not, "[In the United States], most of these children [the victims of sexual molestation] are between eight and thirteen years old, boys as well as girls. Half are molested within the family and half are molested by non-familial assailants." (Lester, 134.)

Sexual molestation is a problem not only in the secular society, but within the Christian community as well. Alice Huskey points out how widespread sexual abuse is (in the United States):

"In a group of four friends, one may have been abused. In a school or church classroom or Bible study of twenty, five may be victims of abuse. In a church of two hundred, fifty may be victims of abuse. In a workplace of fifty, twelve may have been abused. Five hundred individuals may be direct victims of sexual abuse in a small community of two thousand. If you attend a family reunion of one hundred close relatives, twenty five could be sexual abuse victims."[9]

As we have already seen, the statistics are much higher (and much lower) in other countries around the world.

You and I must reach out to these women who suffer from the pain of childhood sexual abuse. We, as our sisters' keepers, must reach out with needed help. We must not be startled by the statistics. We must be educated about how to respond, how to help.

---

9   Huskey, p. 36.

WHAT HAPPENS WHEN A GIRL IS SEXUALLY ABUSED?
In *Daughters Without Dads*, Lois Mowday writes: "Victims of sexual abuse may develop sexual problems that may be acted out in opposite ways: promiscuity or asexuality. ... Numerous problems may result from sexual abuse: eating disorders, low self-esteem, difficulty establishing and maintaining healthy relationships, trouble coping with stressful situations, inability to grow in maturity, and blocked spiritual growth.

"Therapy can be beneficial, but a daughter and her abusing father seldom reach a healing in their damaged, twisted relationship. Sexual abuse is such a horrifying violation of the woman that it is almost impossible to erase the damage done. Forgiveness can happen, but it is usually communicated between the involved parties and God—not between daughter and abusing father."[10]

OTHER FORMS OF CHILD ABUSE
Sexual abuse is not the only abuse children may suffer at the hands of parents or relatives. They may also endure physical abuse, emotional abuse, and parental neglect.

Not until 1871 did a group form in the United States that opposed child abuse. In 1866, when Mary Ellen Wilson was abused by her adoptive parents, the American Society for the Prevention of Cruelty to Animals intervened!

Child abuse can come in many forms:

Physical abuse: Slapping, pushing, kicking, shoving

---

10   Lois Mowday, *Daughters Without Dads* (Nashville: Oliver Nelson, 1990), p. 24.

and injuring in other non-accidental ways. Physical abuse can be mild or it can be deadly.

Emotional abuse: Degrading, rejecting, and threatening a dependent youngster. It may be withholding love and affection or using hateful words that destroy self-confidence.

Child neglect: The child's basic physical, emotional, or spiritual needs are not met or parental love is not provided.

The National Center on Child Abuse and Neglect (in the U.S.) estimates that "one million children are abused each year, resulting in two thousand deaths."[11]

Children are to be loved, cared for, and physically, mentally, emotionally, and spiritually nurtured. Children require adults to help them, advise them, and guide them into adulthood. No parent is perfect, and many parents face difficult circumstances; but that's no excuse for hurting a child. A distressful childhood can overshadow, and even ruin, an entire lifetime.

A hurt child will often grow into an adult who has no sense of self-worth. Without this important sense of self-worth, a person may be emotionally maimed for life.

Liz has also been the victim of another type of child abuse—parental abandonment. Every child's unspoken fear is to be abandoned, either emotionally or physically, by a primary caregiver.

More and more women today are carrying the burdens of childhood trauma. These burdens are affecting their marriages, their parenting, and their

11   Cheryl McCall, "The Cruelest Crime," *Life*, December 1984, p. 58.

jobs. We are made aware daily of how immature, selfish, and/or addictive behavior (such as behavior caused primarily by alcohol, sex, pornography, gambling, or drugs) are tearing apart our world's families and breaking the hearts of our children—children who grow into adulthood with severe problems.

We call these families *dysfunctional families*. They usually cannot give adequate physical, emotional, and spiritual guidance to their children. Growing up in a dysfunctional family can cause a lifetime of sorrow, problems, and general grief. Most often, the children of these unhealthy families will produce unhealthy families of their own.

Hurting Women

Is healing of childhood wounds possible, even wounds caused by sexual, emotional, or physical abuse? Can adult victims of childhood trauma find wholeness for their broken hearts and crushed spirits? Listen to Liz.

"Yes, healing is possible. We can recover hope. God can heal open wounds that fester with anger and hate. When Jenny [her Christian counselor] reached out to me, she helped me to understand that I was not at fault in the abuse. Jenny prayed with me and helped me to understand that God could so fill my heart and mind with his love, his forgiveness, and his strength, that I could find healing in him even in the midst of my greatest struggles."

Liz reached out to Jenny. Jenny reached out to Liz. And both Christian women reached out to the Lord. Liz received the healing she sought.

What was the primary discovery Liz made about God's healing? Over a period of time God revealed to Liz that she could forgive her father for his actions toward her. She discovered what every woman abused in childhood can discover: Complete forgiveness comes directly from God and is the major force in emotional healing. The Holy Spirit gives us the power to forgive those who have caused us pain— not to *excuse* them for their actions, but to *forgive them* willingly. Forgiveness has the power to relieve us from the pain of memories, to provide us once again with strength and joy in our lives.

What exactly is forgiveness? Lewis B. Smedes writes: "Forgiveness is God's invention for coming to terms with a world in which...people are unfair to each other and hurt each other deeply."[12]

Perhaps my favorite definition of forgiveness is this one, by Dr. Ray Burwick: "Bear the reality of the hurt, then choose to remember it against him (or her) no longer. The person who forgives faces completely the extent of hurt or wrong dealt to him. He doesn't rationalize for it or for the person who offended him. He doesn't block it out of his mind. He doesn't cover or mask it with alcohol, drugs, shock treatments, or a life-style of busy-ness. He sets the offender free from the wrong and wipes the slate clean."[13]

A clean slate. Only through the power of the Holy Spirit can an abused woman truly forgive those who are impossible to forgive and wipe the slate clean.

---

12 Lewis B. Smedes, *Forgive and Forget: Healing the Hurts We Don't Deserve* (New York: Harper & Row, Publishers, 1984), pp. xi-xii.

13 Ray Burwick, *The Menace Within: Hurt or Anger* (Homewood, AL: Ray Burwick), p. 93.

You and I must show hurting women how, through the Holy Spirit, to wipe the slate clean and begin a new life.

WHO IS THE HURTING WOMAN?

So often we don't know her name. We only know that she is a woman with a dreadful secret, a secret that lives in her heart and mind every day. She is embarrassed about her secret pain. For years she has suffered with it. She is the woman who smiles on the outside and churns on the inside. She's your next door neighbor. She sits beside you during church worship services. She's your mother, your daughter, your granddaughter, your best friend. She is your spiritual sister, and she's hurting. She needs a healing touch, someone who reaches out with the help she needs.

You and I must introduce her to the Healer. We must encourage her to reach out to Jesus in faith. Like the woman who touched Jesus' robe, she can find wholeness. She can speak the words the woman of many years ago may have spoken:

"To my surprise, his voice was gentle. 'Daughter,' he said to me. I looked up into his eyes. He called me 'daughter,' as if I actually belonged to him, to his family. It had been a long time since anyone had so lovingly, so purely, called me 'daughter.'

"He continued. 'Your faith has healed you. Go in peace and be freed from your suffering.'

"Devastation, shame, humiliation. All of these were gone from my life. I trusted Jesus with my painful secret. I reached out to Him, and He reached back to me with the love, help, and healing I needed most."

7

with love

Helping mothers of suicide victims

| Bible Study: Read Luke 7:11-16 |

When death claims the person that a woman loves, she will go through a period of deep mourning. This time in life can be difficult, if not devastating. Overnight the loss of a loved one can dramatically change her life. She needs someone at that time to reach out to her with love. We've all been "there," and we remember with gratitude the spiritual sisters who reached out to us.

Grieving women have said that the death of a child is the most difficult for them to bear. One woman described that when her healthy child died from a car accident, she grieved primarily because of the lost potential that child's untimely death represented. She also desperately missed the child. She held a deep vacuum in her heart for that absent child.

Throughout history, mothers have had to deal with the untimely deaths of their children. I have a photograph of my grandmother, as a little girl in 1905, holding in her arms her dead newborn sister. My grandmother's young face, stained with tears, speaks volumes.

The first mother, Eve, lost a son to untimely death. Women have lost children through disease, accident, murder, and suicide.

Let's consider the poor widow who lived in Nain at the time of Jesus. She had already lost her husband to death. We aren't told how her only son died, but she stood by his coffin and painfully mourned his untimely death. Perhaps he died of a disease untreatable in that day. Perhaps he died from an accident. No doubt, this son provided the livelihood for himself and his mother.

When Jesus walked into Nain that day, he saw the grieving mother standing beside her son's dead body during the funeral. The emotional sight moved Jesus. It stirred his heart. Luke tells us "when the Lord saw her, his heart went out to her" (Luke 7:13).

Jesus stopped and put his hand on the coffin, a definite taboo among the religious people of his day. No person of God was allowed to touch the dead, for the dead were proclaimed unclean. Jesus reached out to the corpse. To the shock of the crowd, Jesus spoke to the dead man, "Young man, I say to you, get up!" (v. 14).

Scripture paints the unforgettable portrait: "Jesus gave him back to his mother!" (v. 15). In this mother's greatest time of need, Jesus reached out to her with love, with compassion, and with the gift of her son's life.

Unlike Jesus, you and I cannot give a dead child back to a grieving mother. But we can reach out to her in the way Jesus often reached out to those who grieved the loss of a loved one. With love and compassion, we can give her Jesus' hope. We can tell her that Jesus not only reached out in love to a nameless widow at Nain, but he is alive today, and he can reach out to her in her deepest pain.

Only a short while after Jesus journeyed to Nain, he journeyed to Calvary. While the widow at Nain rejoiced in the company of her resurrected son, Jesus' mother stood and grieved beside Jesus' dead body. To the amazement of his mother and friends, however, three days later Jesus came back to life. Jesus' resurrection from the dead gives us hope of eternal life in him.

GRIEF THAT ALMOST NEVER ENDS

When a mother loses a child to death, she also loses that child's future. She carries that child with her all her life. The mother might think, "He would be a senior in high school, planning to enter college next year." "What would she look like as an adult?" The child is always growing up; the mourning never really ends.

Her son is the little one she nursed as a baby. With tears in her eyes, she sent him off to first grade toting his new book bag. He is the one for whom she stood and cheered at his Saturday morning soccer games.

113

Her daughter is the little one she held all night waiting for the fever to break. This is the child she shopped with for her first white Easter shoes. When she played her first piano recital piece, this loving mother proudly clapped and told the mother seated beside her: "That's my daughter!"

A mother is devastated when an accident takes the life of her child. She sits by the hospital bed and prays for the child who is dying from disease. She experiences shock and intense anger when someone without conscience purposely takes the life of her child.

The young high school graduate from Mountain Brook, Alabama, Natalie Holloway, lived only minutes from my house. She disappeared in 2005 while on a graduation trip with her senior class to Aruba. Her anguished mother, Beth Twitty, heard rumors that her daughter had been murdered, or that Natalie had been sold to sex traffickers. She searched for her daughter for years in Aruba, and finally stated: "I've just prayed for an answer, and that's all I've ever wanted. I've just wanted an answer to what happened."[1] Natalie is presumed dead, but the case is still unsolved.

As difficult as these murders and deaths are to accept, they aren't the most difficult. There is one kind of death that is so needless, so untimely, so horrifying that words fail to describe a parent's grief. That devastating death is suicide by a child's own hand.

---

1   Found at: http://www.nypost.com/p/news/regional/item_2yj2zUH Wyz3iRSC0K5N1qJ;jsessionid=B053A965D2D1C53A955571033F23A92F. Accessed: 1/30/10.

A Child's Death by Suicide

Memories that used to bring such beautiful thoughts instead will be agents of pain and confusion when a child commits suicide. The question "why?" will be a constant companion. "The grief after suicide is one of the most difficult grief persons ever experience. And the grief almost never ends, although its intensity diminishes," Bill Blackburn writes in his book *What You Should Know About Suicide.*[2]

Suicide used to be only whispered about when the victim's family wasn't in sight. Our society has opened up to the pain and problem of suicide. Suicide prevention, and care for families experiencing suicide, are coming to the forefront of our society.

Never has the epidemic of suicide become more prevalent in our world among our young people. In the United States, for instance, youth suicide now takes second place as the major cause of death among young people.[3]

Consider the problem:

Every year, almost one million people die from suicide; a "global" mortality rate of 16 per 100,000, or one death every forty seconds.

In the last forty-five years suicide rates have increased by 60 per cent worldwide.

Suicide is among the three leading causes of death among those aged 15-44 years in some countries, and the second leading cause of death in the 10-24 years age group. (These figures do not include suicide

---

2   Bill Blackburn, *What You Should Know About Suicide* (Dallas: Word Publishing, 1990), p. 143.

3   Bill Blackburn, Ibid., p. 29.

attempts, which are up to twenty times more frequent than *completed* suicide.)

Although traditionally suicide rates have been highest among the male elderly, rates among young people have been increasing to such an extent that they are now the group at highest risk in a third of countries, in both developed and developing countries.

Mental disorders (particularly depression and alcohol use disorders) are a major risk factor for suicide in Europe and North America; however, in Asian countries impulsiveness plays an important role. Suicide is complex with psychological, social, biological, cultural, and environmental factors involved.[4]

The World Health Organization (WHO) reports that approximately every forty seconds, another family loses a loved one to suicide. Most frequently it is associated with psychological factors, such as the difficulty of coping with depression, inescapable suffering or fear, or other mental disorders and pressures. A suicide attempt is often a cry for help and attention, or an expression of despair and the wish to escape, rather than a genuine intent to die. A recent WHO study shows that young people are often at risk, and that suicide is the second largest cause of mortality in the 10-24 age group.[5]

The problem is so extreme, that each year the world holds a "World Suicide Prevention Day" on September 10th each year as an initiative of the International

---

4   Found at: http://www.who.int/mental_health/prevention/suicide/sui-cideprevent/en/. Accessed: 1/29/10.

5   Found at: http://www.ncbi.nlm.nih.gov:80/pmc/articles/PMC1472267/. Accessed: 1/29/10.

Association for Suicide Prevention (IASP). It is co-sponsored by the World Health Organization (WHO). The theme in 2009 was "Suicide Prevention in Different Cultures." Begun in 2003, the purpose of World Suicide Prevention Day is to improve education about suicide, disseminate information, decrease stigmatization and, most importantly, raise awareness that suicide is preventable. This year's World Suicide Prevention Day involved thousands of participants in hundreds of locations in over forty countries around the world.[6]

What country holds the record for the highest number of youth suicides? The Russian federation, and it is followed by Lithuania, Finland, Latvia, and Slovenia. Sweden (which can be compared with the U. S.) is, according to this list, in 18th place. At the bottom of the list are Great Britain, Spain, Portugal, Italy, and last Greece.[7]

In this chapter we will directly confront the problem of suicide among our youth. We need to learn how to reach out to the woman who has been hurt by the suicidal death of her child. We also need to learn about warning signs, and how they can lead to suicide prevention. Both prevention, and care for those affected, are essential to reaching out to women who experience this firsthand.

ELIZABETH'S STORY

Elizabeth, fifteen, left prayer meeting early at her church and walked with a friend to her nearby home.

---

6   Found at: http://www.iasp.info/wspd/. Accessed: 1/29/10.

7   Found at: http://web4health.info/en/answers/bipolar-suicide-statistics. Accessed: 1/29/10.

On the way, Elizabeth told her friend she was going to finish cleaning her room and then kill herself. Thinking Elizabeth was being overly dramatic, her friend didn't take the threat seriously.

At 8:15, Elizabeth's mother came home from church and found her in her room, dead from a self-inflicted gunshot wound.

The youth at church later told the parents that Elizabeth had talked often about killing herself, but subtly and almost jokingly. As early as six years before, Elizabeth had told a friend about finding a gun hidden in her parent's closet.

"We didn't tell any of our five children that we owned a gun," said Carolyn, Elizabeth's mother. "We kept it trigger-locked, unloaded, and hidden in the closet, with the trigger-lock key in another part of the closet."

Elizabeth went to a lot of trouble to find the gun, bullets, and trigger-lock key.

Elizabeth was a pretty girl who was dedicated to the Lord, active in church, successful in school, and musically talented. But Elizabeth had severe physical problems caused by congenital birth defects. She also had undergone major surgery several years before and suffered from chronic back pain. Her physical pain and condition also caused emotional pain.

"It is apparent to us now that Elizabeth had planned her death for some time," said Carolyn. "She made elaborate preparation in her room that Wednesday night. She placed her music awards neatly in a plastic laundry basket, turned photos of herself facedown, laid out clothes for her burial, and left a note."

The note began: "I love you all, and I'm so sorry."

GROPING FOR ANSWERS

We must reach out to those mothers and fathers who have been devastated by the suicidal death of a child. This crisis will test their faith as no other crisis can. Victims admit they turn almost inside out groping for answers, for understanding. "What did we do wrong?" usually is the first question they ask. "How could we have prevented it?" most often is the second question.

We can begin ministering to grieving family members by telling them that the warning signs of suicide are often missed. The signs can be so subtle that even trained counselors can miss them. We can assure the hurting mother that the suicide of a child can happen for many reasons. Most parents who ask: "What did we do wrong?" have done nothing wrong in their parenting. They are not responsible for the death of their child. We all make mistakes in our parenting because we learn parenting as we parent. But few of us make mistakes that lead a child to his or her suicidal death. We need to reach out to the parents with sensitivity to answer those haunting questions they painfully consider, but often do not verbalize.

Going back to work, school, or church after the news of the suicide has spread is intensely difficult. The stigma of suicide is very real, even in our ever-accepting society. Suicide can adversely affect the family members' relationships with one another, friends, co-workers, neighbors, and fellow church members.

"I look into the eyes of my friends, family, neighbors, and fellow church members and wonder what they're thinking about me, about our family, about our parenting," one mother said. "People we have known for years have begun to avoid us, are careful not to make eye contact, and don't know what to say or do."

YOUTH SUICIDE

We've seen how youth suicide is quickly becoming a world epidemic. The five biggest factors leading to suicide are drug abuse, not getting along with parents, peer stresses, problems of growing up, and alcohol abuse. In other countries around the world, the reasons may vary. More than half of teens in the United States admit they know another teen that has completed suicide. It touches all communities around the globe. In our homes, our neighborhoods, and in our churches, untold numbers of moms and dads, brothers and sisters, grandparents, teachers, classmates, and church-mates are grieving the young people who have chosen death over life.

We also grieve when we hear of the ever-increasing problem of school shootings and the suicides of the killers.

As Christian women, you and I can have an effective ministry to women grief-stricken by a child's suicide. Hurting women are everywhere, and they are wondering where they can find relief from the whys and hows. Perhaps the first way we can reach out to them is to seek understanding of the problem of youth suicide.

The Causes

What causes a young person to end his or her life? The reasons vary from country to country, but some contributing factors are:

- loneliness

- isolation

- intense frustration

- depression

- a feeling of worthlessness and/or failure

- drug and alcohol use

- lack of family, lack of family attention and/or family stability

- grief caused by divorce or death of parents

- the loss of a close friend to suicide. This often leads to a "copycat" or "cluster" suicide. According to psychiatrist Faye Doss, once a friend or classmate has committed suicide, suicide becomes a more acceptable alternative. Youth will often romanticize death and deny its finality.

In Elizabeth's case, intense physical and emotional pain motivated her.

Sometimes a young person will feel great pressure to achieve and will fear a possible failure. The high-achieving adolescent, obsessed with grades and success, many feel keen frustration when he or she can't perform to perfection. Suicide may seem an attractive way out.

One study has linked the causes of youth suicide around the world to sexual and emotional abuse, stress, unplanned pregnancy, problems concerning sexual preference, unemployment, imprisonment, and running away from home.[8]

Youth in crisis often perceive their problems as inescapable. They may feel an utter loss of control. During these times, they often cannot think clearly, make decisions, sleep, eat, or work. Most suicide victims don't really want to die, but they can't see a future without pain.

No Community Untouched

Suicide touches every church, every community, every country in the world. Experts predict the problem will increase. You might know someone who has lost a child to suicide. You and I can reach out in love.

Adolescent suicide most often is not a spur-of-the-moment decision. It comes after long-term feelings of depression, confusion, helplessness, and hopelessness. Yearning for freedom from deep emotional pain can drive youth to seek relief. Too often in their quest for peace and rest, youth choose this permanent solution.

What can you and I do? We can help our spiritual sisters watch their children for suicidal warning signs. We can intervene when possible. Some warning signs are subtle; we may not even notice them. Other warning signs shout to be heard; but, even so, we may miss them.

---

8   Found at: http://www.unicef.org/pon96/insuicid.htm. Accessed: 1/29/10.

Suicidal symptoms in young people may include:

- irregular patterns in eating and sleeping
- changes in behavior, such as a sudden cheerfulness after a time of depression
- withdrawal from family, friends, and social activities
- a preoccupation with death and dying
- an increase in alcohol and/or drug use
- decreased interest in personal appearance
- lack of interest in hobbies, work, school, or other usual activities
- talking about committing suicide, or emailing/ texting about committing suicide.
- giving away prized possessions and beginning to prepare for death.

Bullying also causes young people to end their lives. They see no way to escape the day by day bullies at school. In 2009, in Springfield, MA, Carl Joseph Walker-Hoover, only eleven years old, came home from school and hanged himself. The children at school bullied him, told him he acted like a girl, and called him "gay." Finally, the boy could take the bullying no more. He left a note, saying he loved his mother and his aunt. He left his Pokemon games and cards to his six-year-old brother. And he hanged himself from the railing of the third-floor landing by an electrical cord, while his mother prepared the family's supper. "I know he would not have done this," his mother said, "unless he felt he did not have any other choice."[9]

In the U. S., suicide rates among youths aged 15-24 have tripled in the past half-century, even as rates for adults and the elderly have declined. And for every youth suicide completion, there are nearly 400 suicide attempts.[10]

The world has also recently seen the suicidal results of *cyber bullying*. Cyber bullying is defined by the Center for Safe and Responsible Use of the Internet (CSRIU) as, "being cruel to others by sending or posting harmful material or engaging in other forms of social cruelty using the Internet or other digital technologies, including cell phones." It also has various forms including both direct and indirect activities to damage or interfere with the relationship of the student being targeted such as posting, impersonation, or disseminating personal information or images.

The recent suicide of 12-year-old Sarah Butler, an Arkansas seventh grader, has once again brought attention to the need for more aggressive cyber bullying legislation.

Butler hung herself at her family home, after being bullied on a popular social networking site by two local youths. Many believe the two youths should be held accountable in some way for her death. The

---

9   Found   at: http://www.boston.com/news/local/massachusetts/articles/2009/04/20/constantly_bullied_he_ends_his_life_at_age_11/. Accessed: 1/29/10.

10   Found at: http://www.canadiancrc.com/Youth_Suicide_in_Canada.aspx. Accessed: 1/29/10.

girl's mother, Starr Chapps, appeared on a television news program in an emotional attempt to make the public aware of this growing concern. Chapps said she saw no signs of distress in her daughter before her daughter's suicide.

In 2006, 13-year-old Megan Meier, of O'Fallon, MO, killed herself after being bullied on MySpace.[11]

In 2009, an Australian youth, Chanelle Rae, fourteen, was the fourth student at her school to complete suicide within a five month period! Chanelle took her own life after apparently being bullied on the internet. Chanelle's mother, Karen, bluntly told the press: "I want to tell people to keep their kids off the rotten internet, it's a horrible place."[12]

Numerous other children around the world have reported acts of cyber bullying.

Before we allow parents to start blaming themselves for their child's suicide, let us help them understand how difficult society makes it for a parent and for a young person these days. Life demands much from a parent. In the exhausting day after day task of parenting; with the increasingly difficult job of keeping the family fed and sheltered; by sheer time, energy, and work demands a mother or father cannot be totally attentive toward the child. This is especially true if they have more than one child in the family. Parenting is a tough job. Sometimes even when parents do their best, something happens.

---

11   Found at: http://www.areawidenews.com/story/1591912.html. Accessed: 1/29/10.

12   Found at: http://www.heraldsun.com.au/news/hundreds-of-mourners-gather-for-chanelle-raes-funeral/story-0-1225754338127. Accessed: 1/29/10.

Parents must also realize they are not their children's only influence. Our society makes it difficult to rear a child. Our children are shaped and influenced by a culture addicted to sex, money, drugs, alcohol, gambling, the occult, and violence. Murder, sex, and crime in general often are sensationalized by newspapers, radio, television, and films.

Sometimes parents are alerted to suicidal warning signs, but often a parent can fail to understand the signals until after the suicide has happened. Only in looking back do the pieces of the puzzle seem to fit together and show a true picture of the situation.

A LOVING, CARING CHURCH

Friends and concerned church members can sometimes step in and rescue the child from suicide. Sometimes, however, they cannot. The death occurs. The ministry and love we show the parents and other family members can make a great difference in their lives.

Elizabeth's family decided they should actively work to prevent other suicides. Word spread throughout the church the Wednesday night after her death. The pastor called a special meeting for the congregation. Counselors from a local high school and the city's crisis center gathered at the church to speak and to counsel with the large group assembled there.

One high school counselor said about that night, "the mood was tense, somber, and serious. Some of the kids were hysterical and blamed themselves for Elizabeth's death."

The next night, the church offered a course in suicide prevention for the entire church family. A week later Elizabeth's parents talked with the youth, parents, and friends at church about her death.

If a family in your church has experienced the suicide of a child, talk to your pastor and/or church staff. Even though this is an intensely personal crisis they are facing, minister to the family as Christ's representatives.

A Message of Hope

Following is a letter Elizabeth's mother wrote several months after Elizabeth's death. Perhaps you can share this letter with a mother who grieves over the death of her child. It contains a message that holds many answers for those experiencing the pain of losing a child.

"In those dark days immediately following Elizabeth's death, I felt as if my very soul had been ripped apart. I felt like an empty shell of my former self; one merely going through the motions of living. At times I could not feel God's presence, the God who had always been there for me. He seemed so silent and distant, and I was too devastated even to pray for myself.

"Yet somehow, in the middle of all this hopelessness and total despair, I began to feel little moments of comfort. The incredible hurt and pain were still there, but I began to feel God's presence again, maybe only for a few fleeting minutes; but I knew He was there, holding me up and walking beside me. Often I would receive a phone call or a note in the mail from a friend who had been praying for our family. Then I would think back on how the burden of pain and grief had seemed miraculously lifted for a time.

"This final thought probably has been the single most comforting things said to me since Elizabeth's death.

"As a Christian I always have believed that God has given us two supreme gifts—our lives and the life of His Son Jesus Christ who was sacrificed for us. I was obsessed with this thought: Would God be angry at Elizabeth for throwing His gift back in His face? Would He forgive her for taking her own life?

"I verbalized this thought to a young man who was a close friend of Elizabeth's. In wisdom which far surpassed his eighteen years, he replied: 'Are you angry at Elizabeth for taking her own life?'

"I replied 'No, of course not.' I knew the physical burden she carried from numerous congenital birth defects, and I knew the additional emotional pain her physical condition created. I ached with her. The burdens she had borne had broken my heart. I could never be angry with her.

"Then he asked: 'Is your husband angry with her?'

"I again replied, 'No.'

"Then he said, 'How much greater and more perfect is her Heavenly Father's love for her than the love of her earthly parents.'

"My question was answered."

8

REACHING

with faithfulness

OUT

Helping women cope with loss and grief

| Bible Study: Read John 20:1-18 |

We know little from Scripture about Mary Magdalene. Luke 8:2 tells us she was a follower of Jesus "from whom seven demons had come out." With demon possession, evil took control of this woman. We can only imagine what torture she must have felt before meeting Jesus. How might she tell us her story today?

"They tormented me night and day, causing me to cry out for rest, for death, for anything that could deliver me from their torture. I could not escape the evil spirits.

"Torment plagued me every waking moment and caused me to threaten and terrorize those in the town I yearned to embrace. Evil spirits growled through my voice, and I blushed at their words. I could not control them; I could not run from them. Madness, insanity, and fierceness became my identity to those I loved most. I could not fight, for I truly believed that evil had won, and I was its eternal victim.[1]

"Then a stranger walked into my life one day. He came to Magdala, the city where I lived. He reached out to me, and with rare authority, ordered the seven demons from me. In an instant, they left. I became the loving woman I had once been. Transformation. I have learned that nothing is too difficult for God to do. I have felt God's presence. I have seen God's mighty love and faithfulness.

"Jesus, you reached out to me. You released me from the agonizing grip and pain of evil. You have given me a new identity—your identity. You have given me a new life, a life in you. Please allow me to reach back to you. I will give you all I have to give, my love, my loyalty. I promise never to leave your side. I will follow you even to the ends of the earth."

FAITHFUL FOLLOWER

Mary Magdalene followed Jesus faithfully throughout his ministry. She became a vital part of the small group of women who traveled with Jesus and ministered to him and his disciples.

When Roman soldiers arrested Jesus and his followers fled with fear, Mary stayed with him.

When they nailed Jesus to the wooden cross, and left him to die, Mary knelt at his pierced feet.

---

1 See *Holman Bible Dictionary*, "Demon Possession." The behaviors described are typical of demon possession, although we have no proof from Scripture that Mary Magdalene suffered from any or all of these behaviors.

When they placed Jesus' body within a rock-hewn tomb, Mary crept through predawn darkness to envelop him with fragrant spices.

She followed Jesus to the ends of the earth, to the cross, to his death, and to the grave.

Jesus rewarded Mary's devotion. He reached out to her. Jesus healed Mary, he saved her, he gave her new life. Jesus encouraged Mary, he taught her, he shared with her the secrets of God. Jesus gave her purpose and hope and restored her girlhood dreams. And, finally, Jesus chose Mary. From among all his followers, Jesus of Galilee chose Mary of Magdala to announce his greatest victory, his victory over evil, his resurrection from the grave.

Imagine her excitement upon finding the stone moved from the tomb and the Lord alive!

"I have seen the Lord!" she shouted to the small band of bewildered disciples who still cowered in fear and deeply mourned the death of their leader.

"I have seen the Lord!" Mary continues to shout through Scripture—through the ages—to you, to me, and to unknowing millions of women around the world.

THE PAIN OF LOSS

How often, during the course of life's journey, do you and I confront the effects of evil face-to-face? Evil somehow changes us. Evil affects us personally through our loved ones—their betrayals, their unkind actions. Evil affects us as a world society. We heard the word "evil" used numerous times among news commentators on September 11, 2001. It referred to the terrorists who hijacked commercial airliners, flew them into New York's World Trade Center and other locations, and killed thousands of people.

Evil can torment us night and day physically, emotionally, mentally, and spiritually. We encounter trials every day. We lose a spouse to death or a marriage to disaster. We lose a child to gangs, to cults, to drugs. We lose vitality and youth. We suffer as cancer, leukemia, or AIDS destroys the healthy bodies of those we love. We experience a world tragedy caused by human hands, a terrorist attack, a bombing, an act of genocide. Evil is an inevitable part of life on Earth. We fear it, but we cannot always stop it.

Someone you know, someone you love, someone in your church or neighborhood or community—someone may be hurting at this moment due to the results of evil.

Reach out to her, as a spiritual sister, who cares. She needs your faithful assurance, your faithful touch. She needs to know that God is near, even when she asks her difficult questions of faith.

"Why, Lord?" we hear the women around us ask. These are the women in our world who suffer loss—a loved one, a job, a home, a spouse, etc. "Why do you allow such terrible losses in our lives?" these women ask. "Your Word tells us you love us. Your Word tells us you are all powerful. If you love us, if you can protect us and those we love, then why don't you?"

It's an honest, heart-felt question—an eternal question we have all asked at one time or another in our lives. "Why, Lord?" we hear the women around us ask. The question echoes down through the centuries, and never seems to be answered in a satisfactory way.

SANDY'S STORY

I remember years ago taking my daughter, Alyce, to her first day of kindergarten. That day Alyce and I met five-year-old Sandy and her grandmother. Alyce and Sandy had the same teacher. During the twenty minutes I stayed with Alyce, I noticed that little Sandy never smiled. With tears in her eyes, and away from Sandy's hearing range, her grandmother spoke in hushed tones to the teacher. I knew something was wrong, but not until Alyce and Sandy became best friends did I learn the reason for the whispering and sadness.

A few months before school had started, Sandy, her baby sister, and her mother and father were driving home from vacation. In the middle of a busy intersection, a speeding car ran the red light and struck their car broadside. The mother and father were killed instantly. A nearby trucker witnessed the crash and sprang from his truck to rescue Sandy and her sister, both of whom by some miracle were not seriously hurt. He quickly pulled Sandy from the wreckage and placed her into the arms of concerned onlookers. Then he turned and ran toward the crying baby still strapped in her infant seat. But just as he approached the car door, the car burst into flames, leaving no hope of rescue.

THE MYSTERY

Why does God permit such horrible things to happen to people? What good can come out of these sad and senseless deaths? "Why?" is a question that philosophers, theologians, Christians, and children have cried out to God in deepest pain. This question can so quickly turn people away from God. Evil seems the victor.

Recently, I read the Holocaust diaries of a Russian woman. She wrote these diaries as a young girl, living in Ukraine. She had a happy life with a large loving family. Then Hitler and his German army, during World War II, invaded Ukraine and Russia. A German soldier killed her father. This young girl and her mother ended up on a German train that took them to a labor camp in Germany.

After the war, with her family members lost and/ or murdered, the girl, Nonna, traveled to the United States. She met a man, fell in love, and married. She became a wife and mother of three children. But her Holocaust story was so painful, she kept her secret and hid her Holocaust diaries. After more than a half-century of marriage, she finally told her husband and children her remarkable story. Nonna spent the rest of her life searching for her family members, but never found them. (Read Nonna's story in *The Secret Holocaust Diaries: The Untold Story of Nonna Bannister*, published by Tyndale House Publishers, Spring, 2009. Co-authors: Carolyn Tomlin and Denise George.)

When I think of "evil," I immediately think of cruel leaders like Hitler. Why does God allow the Hitlers of the world to maim, murder, steal? I don't know. Reading Nonna's diaries broke my heart.

My friend, author Carolyn Tomlin, and I put Nonna's diaries in print so that the whole world could read her story. Even though stalked by evil and tragedy, Nonna kept her strong faith in God. She shows us extraordinary courage while even in the grip of evil itself. People across the world have read the book, and tell us that God touched their hearts through Nonna's story.

Sometimes evil seems the victor. I look around at the lives of my spiritual sisters, and I see such unexplainable loss and hurt.

Ellen still has nightmares about her childhood as the victim of an evil, incestuous father.

Carrie still suffers the guilt of a long-ago abortion.

Peg, a retired minister's wife, has suffered a lifetime of devastating back pain since her car accident as a newlywed.

Jan, a wife and mother of three small boys, was abandoned and left emotionally and financially hurting by an irresponsible husband.

Cherrie, a young mother of two, has just learned she has terminal cancer and only a few months to live.

Brenda confides she struggles day after day with an alcoholic and abusive husband who won't seek professional help.

Linda, a 40-year-old woman, is trying to understand and cope with the trauma of a broken marriage and rearing teenage boys by herself.

Cheryl experienced betrayal by a best friend, a friend who broke her heart.

Pat, a 28-year-old, has just lost her young husband from an unexpected heart attack.

Laura, a single young woman, was the victim of rape.

Susan, the mother of a toddler, lost her husband in a terrorist-plotted plane crash.

Margie, a single mother, has just lost her job and has no money and no prospects for another job.

Cindy, a young woman with a splintered spine, will spend the rest of her life confined to a wheelchair.

Kelly is deeply hurt to discover her son's homosexual lifestyle.

Adrian's only daughter has just been diagnosed HIV-positive.

Deep loss. Evil face-to-face. These women are hurting. They are our spiritual sisters. I AM my sister's keeper. Many are trying to understand, trying to cope, trying to figure out the *whys* of life. And they are asking the difficult questions of God.

A SUFFERING WORLD OF WOMEN

The daily problems and crises women face today can stagger the imagination. Life is so fragile, and our love for those closest to us can run so deep. What affects those we love—our spouse, children, parents, friends, fellow church members, neighbors—can cause us to suffer too. When we love others, we hurt when they hurt; we grieve when they grieve. As Christian women, our hearts ache with a world that suffers. How often do we bow our heads, weep, and pray for someone we may not know, but with whom we share the pain of life, experience, and loss.

Jesus was there for Mary Magdalene when she faced the evil of seven demons that tormented her. Mary Magdalene was there for Jesus when he faced the cross and death. When each experienced unbelievable pain and most needed a loyal friend, the other was there to reach out with the deep bond of friendship and faithfulness.

Perhaps it is in friendship and faithfulness that you and I can reach out to women who have been hurt by the sting of loss, the devastation of evil, the confusion of tragedy.

Betty's Story

Betty's youngest son, Mark, was addicted to cocaine. One day he left home "his clothes wet from perspiration and the weather severely cold." The evil of drugs had stolen him from her. She never heard from him again.

Betty wrote:

"As I look back now, I believe that deep in my heart I knew he would not come back, but I couldn't face that then. My whole being agonized over him. I knelt on the floor in my kitchen that first night he was gone and cried to the Lord. The next two weeks the trauma was so painful to my mind and emotions I toggled between coping and breaking. During this time the grief and trauma were very evident on my face. I called it the 'death look.'

"Tormenting thoughts came during the following weeks. Days and weeks began to turn into months. Every time I felt I could not go any longer without hearing from Mark, I prayed, weeping with such intense fervency I would dream about him at night.

"Two years passed. One night I received a call from the sheriff's department. Mark's remains had been found.

"I went through the normal reactions of anger and denial. It was traumatic, much more than I had expected. I thought I had been through it all, but the finality hurt; and I tried to hold on to Mark as long as I could."

ASKING "WHY?"

Evil. Pain. Why does God allow them? The hurting women in this world will ask you and me this question when they confront devastating losses. Perhaps it will be their first question.

In his book *Disappointment with God*, Philip Yancey asks: "Is God unfair? Why doesn't he consistently punish evil people and reward good people? Why do awful things happen to people good and bad, with no discernible pattern?"[2]

God does not cause spouses to be abused, teenagers to kill themselves, or loved ones to die in car crashes. God does not cause our sons and daughters to become addicted to drugs or to die horrible, unexplained deaths. But if God is in control of you and me, then

---

2   Taken from the book *Disappointment with God* by Philip Yancey. Copyright 1988 by Philip Yancey. Used by permission of Zondervan Publishing House.

it stands to reason that he permits these things to happen.

"But why?" is the difficult question, and often our spiritual sisters receive a variety of answers. Some answers are mind-boggling, some are soaked in theological mumbo-jumbo, some are truly not biblically based, and some are just plain preposterous. No doubt, you and I have both heard all these answers.

Often I have wondered if God gets tired of our asking him difficult questions of faith. Can we, the creation, question the Creator?

Elisabeth Elliot, a woman of strong faith in God, knows firsthand about suffering, evil, grieving, and about asking the difficult questions of faith. I had dinner with Elisabeth several years ago. I had read her many Christian books, and it gave me a chance to get to know her personally. She has reached millions of people for Christ through retelling her story. Through her own tragedy, she has spent a lifetime faithfully reaching out to other hurting women.

Elisabeth and her young husband, Jim, were missionaries to the Auca Indians in Ecuador, South America. They had been married only a short time when Jim and four other missionaries were savagely murdered in the Amazon rain forest. They were killed by people they had come to minister to, teach, and help.

In 1958, Elisabeth, her daughter Valerie, and another missionary returned to Ecuador to live and work with the Auca Indians. Five years after her husband's death, Elisabeth returned to the scene where her husband was murdered. She and Valerie were guided to the shallow graves by the natives who had killed the missionaries, the natives who were now converted to Christianity and had become her friends.

As they walked along the river, they stopped at the place where the crime took place. The natives responsible for the deaths described to her what had happened that day. We read her book, *Through Gates of Splendor*, and ask "Why?" Why would an all-powerful and all-loving God allow five missionaries to travel so great a distance to spread the gospel to the Auca Indians, and then permit them to be savagely murdered by the very people they ministered to?

My husband, Timothy, and my son, Christian, met the Auca Indians who actually murdered Jim Elliot. The men are now ministers, and, several years ago attended the conference in Europe, *Amsterdam 2000*.

There are many things God allows to happen that we cannot understand. Why? Because God is God—perfect in every way. We are human—far from perfection, and living in a "fallen" and "broken" world. Our faith in God rests on his nature, character, and Word; not on what we think he should do or allow.

A TRUE FAITH

It may not be what hurting women want to hear, but the only answer we can give our spiritual sisters who come to us seeking answers is: God is God. That is the only truth we need to cling to in times of trauma, confusion, and loss. That's the message we need to share with our hurting spiritual sisters. God loves us and allows us to love him or hate him; to trust him or doubt him; to seek him or reject him; and, yes, even to ask him questions.

Perhaps realizing that we do not, and never will, understand is the greatest understanding we can have. We have something very difficult to do in this life, and we must tell other women to do it too. We must trust. We must do the almost impossible.

With faithfulness, we must trust the One we cannot touch and put our arms around to hold, yet the One we know holds our fragile lives and the whole universe.

With loyalty, we must trust the One who died a death we cannot fully comprehend but know has made us right with God and heirs to his family.

With devotion, we must trust the One we cannot audibly hear yet who promises to speak to us if we will listen.

With allegiance, we must trust the One we cannot see yet who lives within us and promises never to leave us. Trusting God to this extent is not easy.

It takes a tough faith to believe that God came to earth, died, and raised himself from death. No wonder the birth, life, death, and resurrection of Jesus Christ are stumbling stones in the path of those who don't believe. They are not logical! We are told to believe scientific and technological impossibilities (such as the virgin birth, Christ's miracles, and the resurrection) in an age of advanced science and technology.

But with assured faithfulness we must reach out to hurting women and tell them about the One who reached out first to us. Christ's faithfulness led him to a cross.

You and I must believe and share this fact: we don't, and probably never will, understand the whys and ways of God. Until God chooses to reveal his will to us, we can only search, ponder, pray, trust, and continue to seek greater understanding.

In the meantime, God permits us to endure suffering for reasons we do not understand. Perhaps it is a gift to us that God allows us to share with him a broken heart. Scripture tells us that the heart of God has been broken again and again. Perhaps only in our sufferings can God fully come in, pull us closer to Him, and help us understand our lives as we live in Christ.

GOD'S MIGHTY LOVE

The Bettys of this world are all around us. They are the women hurt by evil and loss—the very ones to whom God reaches out through our hearts, through our hands to our hurting spiritual sisters.

Can you imagine the pain Betty endured when she watched evil devastate her son's young body with drugs?

Can you imagine the agony of waiting two years without one word from him?

Can you imagine receiving the call from the sheriff telling Betty her son was dead?

Christian women have reached out to Betty with love, faithfulness, and understanding. Betty has stayed close to her Savior during her long ordeal. Listen to her closing words:

> "I talked with a friend last week who lost her youngest son three years ago. She said, 'The third

year is the worst. I feel like I will always grieve; it is a part of my identity.'

"My heart rejected that statement. I grieved for many years over my son. I fought for his life, and I grieved as I saw him being pulled away from me by drugs. I grieved when I saw him change from a sweet, lovable kid into a bleary-eyed stranger. I grieved when he dropped out of school and his teenage years were stolen from him. I grieved when he disappeared. I grieved when his remains were found. I grieved at his memorial.

"But I refuse to allow grief to be a part of my identity. When my need was the greatest, God gave me more of himself. When I hurt the most, God revealed more of his presence. I became aware of what Jesus really did on the cross. Nothing is too difficult for God to do—in our hearts, minds, or emotions. He helped me lay aside the past—sins, failures, wounds, and grief. Peace over Mark has filled my heart. Thoughts of him no longer consume my days. I have felt God's presence with me. I have seen God's mighty love and faithfulness."

THE "FOREVER PAIN"

Do you know someone who is tormented by the "forever pain"—the pain that is buried so deeply we think we never will be delivered from it?

You and I have a message for the wounded women of this world who cope with the "forever pain." Let us reach out to them and tell them that evil need not win control in their lives. Let us tell them that the battle already has been fought on a cross at Calvary. Jesus has conquered the Evil One. Evil can no longer claim eternal victims.

Let us tell these women that God's mighty love and faithfulness can heal their pain and deliver them from their torment. Nothing is too difficult for the Lord. Just as he reached out to Mary Magdalene, he can reach out to these women and bring healing. They can be freed from demons that claw at them, twist their thoughts, and destroy their beautiful memories.

Jesus Christ can give the woman, hurt by loss and evil, a new identity, a new life. For he is the One who is faithful. Eternally faithful.

REACHING

with God's eternal hope

OUT

Helping women find hope in Christ

| Bible Study: Read John 4:4-42 |

This is a message to take to your own heart and to share with all those spiritual sisters who hurt.

This morning, I awoke early and looked out the dining room window. It is autumn in Birmingham, Alabama, my favorite city, and my favorite time of year. The mountains around my home are covered with trees, and the trees sparkle with colorful leaves. I blink my eyes to make sure that the glowing world of emerald, gold, and ruby around me is real. Clouds of mist have nestled into the mountain valleys beneath a sky we might call gray, but that C. S. Lewis would call "silver, dove, and pearl."

Winter will be here soon. The leaves will wither, brown, and die. The freezing rains, sleet, and snow will bury us in their seeming grip of death.

But when winter comes, and all seems dark and cold and gloomy, we can be sure that spring is not far behind. We can look forward to the budding trees and blooming flowers that we know will burst forth into the warmth and beauty of summer. New life. Abundant life. That is our hope, and we can depend on it.

Isn't life somewhat like the seasons? Beneath the tragedies and sorrows of life, beneath thick facial masks that hide our pain, beneath the anxieties, hurts, and broken dreams, the seeds of hope live on. God has placed in each of us the vision of forever. God planted deep within our hearts the hope of home. And hope—for the believer in Jesus Christ—never dies.

NEW HOPE

We live in a world that makes life difficult for women. In some countries, women and their families have been displaced by genocide, by ruthless rulers who maim and murder. In other countries, like present day Haiti, national tragedies—an earthquake—have destroyed lives and property. Around the world, divorce and spouse abandonment have torn apart the cords of marriage and commitment. Women and children are enduring physical, emotional, and mental abuse every day. A dark hopelessness shadows the hearts of many of our young people around the world and leads them to suicide. Sex trafficking and

Internet porn have created horrible situations for girls and women, and it grows increasingly alarming with each new day. Financial collapse ruins families and dreams.

We live in a world of terrorism, where any day might bring an unexpected explosion and death. Evil and hatred seem to be gaining loyal new followers.

A book like this is not nearly long enough to deal with all the problems women face today. Within these pages, however, we have tried to deal with at least some of the trauma women suffer. I truly believe that Jesus expects us, as dedicated Christian women, to reach out to our spiritual sisters—the world's hurting women who need to know him. They need to know that, in Christ, they can find new life, purpose, and hope.

May you and I fully become our sisters' keepers? May we reach out to hurting women around the world with God's heart and God's hands? Jesus reached out to wounded women in his day. He set the example you and I are to follow. Jesus shows us how to reach out with affirmation, love, faithfulness, needed help, God's truth, forgiveness, prayer, and compassion. Surely, life on this planet is not easy. Let us reach out to wounded women everywhere and introduce our hurting spiritual sisters to Jesus, for he, and only he, is the hope that never dies, God's eternal hope.

BIBLE STUDY SECTION:

*Questions for personal reflection
and/or group discussion*

CHAPTER 1: REACHING OUT WITH GOD'S TRUTH

Helping Women Heal from Broken Relationships

Bible Study on John 4:4-42

1. Reread John 4:4-42. Consult a Bible dictionary for help with the following questions:

   Why did Jesus travel through Sychar?

   Why was it unusual for a woman to come to Jacob's well at noon instead of morning?

   What social rules did Jesus break by speaking to a woman? A Samaritan woman? A woman with a bad reputation?

   Why did Jews not associate with Samaritans?

   What did Jesus mean by this statement: "Whoever drinks the water I give him will never thirst"? (v. 14)

   Jesus knew that woman had no husband. Why did he tell her to "go, call your husband and come back"? (v. 16)

   Who did the woman first think Jesus was? (v. 19)

   Why do you think Jesus so plainly revealed himself as the Messiah to the woman? (v. 26)

   What did the woman do immediately after receiving God's truth? Did the Samaritan townspeople believe her? Why? Why do you think Jesus chose the Samaritan woman to take the good news into the town of Samaria?

2. How would you define "forgiveness"?

3. What does Jesus Christ say about forgiveness? Why should we forgive others?

4. Do you believe it is humanly possible to forgive those who have deeply hurt you or someone you love? Why or why not?

5. Can you think of any situation in which you feel you could not forgive another? How does Christ make the difference in the situation? Could you forgive that person in Christ? Explain. Do you think reconciliation is necessary for forgiveness to be complete?

6. How can you best approach a woman hurt by divorce? How can you help her? What can you do in practical ways? How can you minister to her children? How can you help her to begin to forgive in Christlike love?

7. If you have experienced divorce, what are some ways others reached out to you? How can your experience enable you and others to better help those who have been divorced, abandoned, or rejected?

8. Do you believe that "harmony in relationship is the exception, not the rule"? Why or why not? Have you seen this to be true in the lives of other women? Ponder and explain.

9. Investigate ways you and your church can help women and children hurt by the effects of

divorce/abandonment. Investigate how many women in your church or neighborhood are hurting. Ask a Christian counselor for help in starting a divorce recovery workshop in your church or community. You might also consider forming a support group for women near you who have been hurt by divorce.

10. Find out about community support groups for divorced women. Make community support group phone numbers available to your church staff, especially those who work in the area of women's ministry.

Prayer: To close your personal devotional time, or your group discussion time, you may want to use the following prayer:

"Father, teach us how to reach out to wounded women with your truth. Let us direct them to Jesus, who can offer them Living Water so that they will never thirst again.

"We pray for all those women hurt by divorce and abandonment. How it hurts to be rejected by someone we love! Show us how we can show them the importance of forgiveness. We pray that you will be near each wounded woman as she struggles to forgive all those who have hurt her and her children. We pray that she may find a close walk with you, Lord, and that you will heal her and give her new purpose. In Jesus' name, we pray, Amen."

THOUGHTS, REFLECTIONS AND PRAYERS:

_____

_____

_____

_____

_____

_____

_____

_____

_____

_____

_____

_____

_____

_____

_____

_____

_____

_____

_____

_____

_____

_____

_____

_____

_____

_____

_____

_____

_____

_____

_____

_____

_____

CHAPTER 2: REACHING OUT WITH FORGIVENESS

Helping Women Forgive Themselves

Bible Study on John 8:1-11

1. Reread John 8:1-11.

2. Also read Exodus 20:14, Leviticus 20:10, and Deuteronomy 17:5-6 concerning Israel's covenant law that prohibited adultery. What does the law say about punishment for the adulterous woman? Although Scripture does not tell us, in your own opinion, why do you think *the adulterous man* (in John 8: 1-11) did not also face punishment?

3. Think about this statement: "Jesus Christ died on the cross to reconcile us to God. We call it atonement, for in his death, we find 'at-one-ment' with God. We are made right with God." What does this statement mean to you?

4. Consider Acts 23:1. How does this verse relate to Paul's later statement in Romans 8:1: "There is therefore now no condemnation for those who are in Christ Jesus"? How has Paul reacted to the forgiveness offered to him through Christ?

5. Read Psalm 51 and Psalm 103. What statements in these verses show David's acceptance of God's forgiveness?

6. Do you believe that "a forgiven, forgiving, and cleansed heart is the only kind of heart God

can use in his service"? Why or why not? In your opinion, how does a heart filled with self-imposed guilt keep women from doing God's service and ministry?

7. Do you believe God has totally forgiven you of your sin? If so, why? How do you relate to the statement in Jeremiah 31:34 about God's remembering our sins no more? How is forgiving and forgetting possible in our lives as we relate to others?

8. If a dictionary is available, look up the definition of guilt. When is guilt constructive and appropriate? How does the Holy Spirit use guilt in our lives? When is guilt inappropriate? Why is this inappropriate guilt said to be one of Satan's most potent tools? How does he use guilt against us?

9. How can you and I approach women who are not able to forgive themselves? How can we help them to forgive themselves and go on with their lives?

10. What can the church do (and the community) to help wounded women forgive themselves and go on with their lives? Why is this problem more difficult to deal with than other problems, such as spouse abuse, child abuse, and grief? What harm comes to a woman who lives with a lifetime of self-imposed guilt?

Prayer: To close your personal devotional time, or your group discussion time, you may want to use the following prayer:

"Father, please forgive us. Help us to forgive others. And help us to forgive ourselves. Show us how to reach out in forgiveness to hurting women in this world. Allow us to share your Words from Scripture. Allow us to show wounded women, who hurt from their own unforgiven guilt, how to give the load to the Lord and allow him to deal with it for them. In Jesus' name, Amen."

THOUGHTS, REFLECTIONS AND PRAYERS:

_____
_____
_____
_____
_____
_____
_____
_____
_____
_____
_____
_____
_____
_____
_____
_____
_____
_____
_____
_____
_____
_____
_____
_____
_____
_____
_____
_____
_____
_____

CHAPTER 3: REACHING OUT WITH PRAYER

Helping Women Cope with Loneliness

Bible Study on John 11:1-44

1. Reread John 11:1-44.

2. Have you ever been lonely? If so, what did you do about it? What would you now tell others who are lonely?

3. What is the cure for loneliness? How can we make loneliness into a time of solitude and prayer? What is your personal definition of solitude?

4. Why is it important to have a regular daily prayer time and place? Do you personally give prayer the importance Jesus teaches us to give it? How? Have you developed the habit of getting alone with God each day at a regular time and place? Describe.

5. Think about the statement by Myron S. Augsburger: "Paradoxical as it may seem, the true cure for loneliness is to get alone with God, to allow one's self to rest in him. Loneliness is corrected by a sense of belonging to God."

6. Read Jesus' prayer recorded in John 17. For whom does he pray? How does he pray? How did the disciples react to his prayer for them? How do you react to his prayer for you?

7. In John 17, Jesus prays for unity of believers. Have Christian women in general, and have you in particular, worked to bring about unity with the Father and with others? If so, please describe the results.

8. Ponder the following: "Jesus made prayer and fellowship with the Father the priority in his life." In what ways did Jesus make prayer a priority in his life? In what ways can we incorporate his example into our own lives? How can we help other women to realize the priority of prayer in their lives?

9. St. Augustine said: "For Thou has made us for Thyself, and our heart can find no rest until it rests in Thee." Ponder the meaning of his statement: Have you experienced a time when you found rest in God during a troubling time? If so, when? Please describe.

10. James 1:2 tells us, "consider it pure joy…when you face trials of many kinds." How can we be joyful when we feel bereaved, sad, lonely, hopeless? Is it possible? If so, how? How can we help a wounded woman once again find her joy in the Lord?

11. How can we best reach out with prayer to Christian women who suffer? Have you ever thought about beginning a prayer ministry in your church or neighborhood to begin reaching out to others in prayer?

Prayer: To close your personal devotional time, or your group discussion time, you may want to use the following prayer:

> "Father, help us to reach out to hurting women first and foremost with prayer. Help us as we tell wounded women today about the gift of prayer, and the beauty of fellowship with the Father who loves them more than they could ever know. Help them to know that God is just a heart's whisper away, that he yearns for us to seek his presence, that the Father reaches out to them with the gift of prayerful fellowship. Show us how to live our own lives in prayer so that we might be useful to you in your service. In Jesus' name, Amen."

THOUGHTS, REFLECTIONS AND PRAYERS:

_____
_____
_____
_____
_____
_____
_____
_____
_____
_____
_____
_____
_____
_____
_____
_____
_____
_____
_____
_____
_____
_____
_____
_____
_____
_____
_____
_____
_____
_____

Chapter 4: Reaching Out With Compassion

Helping Women Wounded by Discouragement

Bible Study on Luke 13:10-13

1. Describe a person you know who has lost heart, who has lost joy in the Lord, who has forgotten just how much God loves her. How can you and I, as individuals and as a church, minister to her? Why is it important that we do so?

2. Have you ever experienced a situation or a time in your life when you thought God seemed far away? If so, ponder/discuss that time. Have you ever felt that God didn't hear your prayers? If so, describe it.

3. Think about and ponder this statement: "The cycle of loss is a part of everyday living, and loss can often lead to despair, the greatest enemy of the believer's heart." Why, in your opinion, is despair the "greatest enemy of the believer's heart"?

4. Do you believe the "heart can begin again"? What does this statement mean to you?

5. What does Paul's statement mean to you: "God began doing a good work in you. And he will continue it until it is finished when Jesus Christ comes again" (Phil. 1:6 NCV)?

6. If time permits, write a letter (or type an email) to a woman you know who needs a word of hope

in her life. Reach out to her with compassion, just as Jesus reached out to the woman with the crooked back.

Prayer: To close your personal devotional time, or your group discussion time, you may want to use the following prayer:

"O Lord, just as you reached out to the bent-over woman and gave her new hope and new purpose, reach out to us, and allow us to reach out to wounded women everywhere. Teach us by your example how to reach out with compassion. Thank you, dear Lord, for the wounds that you endured at Calvary for us. May we always be grateful to you. May we always remember the price you paid so that we could rest in the new hope you provide. In Jesus' precious name we pray. Amen."

THOUGHTS, REFLECTIONS AND PRAYERS:

_____
_____
_____
_____
_____
_____
_____
_____
_____
_____
_____
_____
_____
_____
_____
_____
_____
_____
_____
_____
_____
_____
_____
_____
_____
_____
_____
_____
_____

CHAPTER 5: REACHING OUT WITH AFFIRMATION

Helping Victims of Spouse Abuse

Bible Study on Luke 7: 36-50

1. What factors in our society, and in our world, contribute to domestic violence? Can we do anything to reduce or eliminate these factors?

2. After years of abuse, Margaret described herself this way: "During those years, I felt so alone, alienated, and worthless. I lost the will to live. I was so under Stephen's control, I couldn't even think for myself. I felt like I didn't belong to the human race." How do you think physical, emotional, verbal, and mental spouse abuse can devastate a person's self-image?

3. Do you think that spouse abuse is too delicate an issue for Christians and churches to intervene? How should you and I deal with a spouse abuse situation we discover in our family, church, or community?

4. How should you and I refer the abused woman to a Christian pastor, attorney and/or counselor?

5. What do words of affirmation do for the woman who has lost her sense of self? Can you think of a time when a friend reached out and affirmed you when you most needed affirmation?

6. As a loving, spiritual sister to the world's abused women, study the signs of spouse abuse, and

learn how to respond to wounded women who ask you for help. What are those signs?

SOME VISIBLE SIGNS OF SPOUSE ABUSE:

If you see one or more of these visible signs of spouse abuse, please suspect some kind of spouse abuse, and alert your pastor or a church/community counselor:

- A woman who has visible cuts, bruises, black eyes, or other injuries and her explanations are not consistent with them. For example, "I ran into a door knob and got this black eye."

- A woman who consistently misses appointments or church commitments.

- Someone who is reluctant to invite anyone to her home.

- One who seems on edge, jittery, withdrawn, or has frequent mood swings.

- A woman who won't stay around to talk with anyone after a luncheon, meeting, or church service because she must always hurry home.

- One who wears unusually heavy clothing out of season, such as long sleeves in hot weather. She may be covering bruises on her arms.

- A woman who often wears makeup heavier than usual to hide bruises or marks on her face.

(Note: If you are meeting with a group, covenant together to pray for God's guidance as you begin to reach out to abused women. Plan together how you can help and affirm an abused woman. Check to see what is available for women in your church and/

or community. Inquire about community programs that can train women to deal directly with battered women and children. Consider starting a support group for battered women in your church.)

OTHER WAYS TO REACH OUT AND HELP AN ABUSED WOMAN: If you suspect spouse abuse, you might consider writing a letter to the wounded woman. You might say something like this:

> "Dear _____: Domestic violence is a delicate issue, but I can no longer ignore the problem. Experts tell me that unless someone intervenes and the violence is stopped, what starts out as a threat, a kick, or a slap will always escalate in intensity. In many cases, a woman's life is in grave danger. In fact, a large percent of women who are killed each year around the world are killed by their spouses. I also have learned that men who batter in one relationship will batter in other relationships. Please forgive me if I am stepping into private territory, but I must take that risk. Please allow me to share some information with you. If you are, indeed, the victim of spouse abuse, seek help immediately. It is never right for someone to hurt you. Know that authorities consider physical abuse to be criminal behavior. Here are steps you can take:
>
> • If you have been hurt or are afraid of being hurt, talk to me, a pastor, or a close friend or family member. Let us help you.
>
> • Make yourself and your children safe. Leave the situation and go to a place of safety. Do not tell the abuser where you are staying.

- Let me help you contact a local women's shelter for support and guidance.

- If your pastor or counselor recommends marital counseling, ask him or her to counsel you separately, not together. Know that a couple in a battering situation need separate counseling. The abuse is his problem, not yours. Your husband is totally responsible for his behavior because he chooses to be abusive. You are not responsible for his behavior. It will put you at greater risk if a pastor counsels you and your abusive husband together. It will take away your freedom of speech, and may lead to more dangerous battering.

I want to help you. Please let me help you. Love, _____ "

CONSIDER HELPING AN ABUSED WOMAN IN THESE WAYS:

- Watch for the warning signs of abuse.

- If you are a close enough friend of the victim, approach her privately, definitely not in the presence of her husband or others. Ask some question that will help her open up to you, such as: "Is everything all right at home?" "Is someone hurting you?" (If her answer is yes, ask: "Is your husband hurting you?")

- Don't judge or criticize her, but listen with understanding, and support her with your prayers, presence, and some concrete suggestions about what she can do.

- Put her in touch with someone who can help her, a pastor, a Christian counselor, and/or your local domestic violence center.

- If she and her children need a safe place to go, take them to a domestic violence safety center, to a family member or friend who lives in another county or state, or to the home of a volunteer in your church who is unknown to the husband and who can offer her a "safe house." (Do not take her into your own home if her husband might anticipate her staying with you. Your life could be endangered.) If possible, help her financially or arrange for the church to provide her with travel and money.

• Know that a woman who is being beaten by a violent husband cannot remain in the home with him. The abuse will not stop. It will accelerate. Until her husband can receive the treatment he needs, she and her children must be removed from the situation.

Prayer: To close your personal devotional time, or your group discussion time, you may want to use the following prayer:

"Dear Lord, we pray for the gift of intuition sensitive enough to penetrate the layers of poise, attractiveness, and charm, to see, hear, and feel the pain that so often hides behind a gentle smile and cheerful voice. We know that beneath the surface sophistication, behind the carefully controlled words and the placid facial expression may reside a tempest of pain and despair.

"Help us to be able to see with your eyes, to hear with your ears, and to feel, to love, to affirm with your heart. Let us be your gentle hands in this hurting world. Draw us near to women who need our help so that we may reach out to them in your name. Amen."

THOUGHTS, REFLECTIONS AND PRAYERS:

CHAPTER 6: REACHING OUT WITH NEEDED HELP

Helping Victims of Childhood Sexual Abuse

Bible Study on Mark 5:21-34

1. How did society in biblical days deal with the hurting woman? How does our society deal with women today who are wounded by terrible secrets? How can we best educate our society and church members to learn about, understand, and reach out to those wounded by painful pasts and show them the way to healing and wholeness?

2. Think about the statement: "Sexual abuse happens in families of all social levels, regardless of income, community prominence, or church affiliation." Do you personally know of a case where sexual abuse happened in a respected family?

3. "Sexual abuse usually leaves its young victim wounded and suffering with a deep sense of shame, guilt, and worthlessness." Why do you think this statement is true?

4. Ponder the following statement: "Sexual abuse is a form of bullying, only worse. A little girl cannot understand this terrible trauma caused by an adult she trusts. She doesn't have the maturity to grasp what is happening to her. She is at the complete mercy of someone older, bigger, smarter. An innocent little girl is no match for an adult abuser." How can we be sensitive to a victim of childhood abuse and how this may affect her image of God as "Father"?

173

5. Think about Alice Huskey's story. In your opinion, did her mother react properly? Why or why not? What would you have done in this case? Do you believe that Alice suffered more from the abuse or from the disclosure of her secret? Alice Huskey writes: "I felt as if I had a big sign around my neck saying 'dirty, ugly, naughty, guilty—stay away.'" Do you believe this is a common feeling among victims of childhood sexual abuse? Why or why not? Does knowing this show you how to better reach out to wounded women, the victims of childhood sexual abuse? Describe.

6. Lois Mowday writes: "Victims of sexual abuse may develop sexual problems that may be acted out in opposite ways: promiscuity or asexuality. ... Numerous problems may result from sexual abuse: eating disorders, low self-esteem, difficulty establishing and maintaining healthy relationships, trouble coping with stressful situations, inability to grow in maturity, and block spiritual growth." How do these problems discourage you in your attempts to reach out to victims of sexual abuse? Do you think you and I can learn to see through to the source of these problems and sincerely reach out with love and help? How?

7. In your opinion, how are the Internet and the growing illegal porn business today hurting girls, teenagers and women, and making them victims of sexual abuse? What do you think can be done to stop this abuse?

8. Investigate support groups in your community who reach out to women who suffer from childhood sexual abuse. Make those phone numbers and addresses available to your church staff, especially those who work in women's ministry. If possible, start a support group in your own church. Bring together women who have been abused and have found healing with women who are still in their struggle to find healing and wholeness.

9. Sexual abuse is only one form of child abuse. Seek more information about child abuse. Learn what you and your church can do about it. If you suspect child abuse occurring in your church or community, talk to your pastor or a trusted member of your church staff. Investigate the situation. If you discover that a child is being abused, work to stop it.

Prayer: To close your personal devotional time, or your group discussion time, you may want to use the following prayer:

"Father, show us how to reach out with needed help to women who have been hurt in childhood by abuse. Bring to those women your healing, your peace, your blessing. Help them to forgive those who have hurt them so that they may find freedom and wholeness. Alert us to children in the world who currently face abuse. Teach us how to recognize abuse and how to help stop it. We know that you love all your children, Lord. Let us be your heart so that we may love them too. Let us be your hands so that we can reach out and offer them needed help. Help us to be true spiritual sisters to others who suffer. In the name of Jesus, the Healer, we pray. Amen."

THOUGHTS, REFLECTIONS AND PRAYERS:

_____
_____
_____
_____
_____
_____
_____
_____
_____
_____
_____
_____
_____
_____
_____
_____
_____
_____
_____
_____
_____
_____
_____
_____
_____
_____
_____
_____
_____

CHAPTER 7: REACHING OUT WITH LOVE

Helping Mothers of Suicide Victims

Bible Study on Luke 7:11-16

1. Ponder this statement: "A child's death is different and more difficult to bear than the death of other loved ones. It means the loss not only of a person, but of a future. … The child is always growing up; the mourning never really ends."

2. Read 1 Corinthians 13. Think about the following:

   • In what ways do we, as Christian women, practice these concepts of love when we reach out to women who need our help?

   • Ponder why Paul might have placed love in a higher category than faith and hope. (See 1 Cor. 13:13).

   • Look up a dictionary definition of love. How does this definition differ from the definition Paul gave in 1 Corinthians 13?

3. Read John 19:25-27. In these verses, John gives us a beautiful relational insight between Jesus, his mother, and his friend. What do these verses show us about the remarkable love of Jesus as he prepared to die? What words would you use to describe this kind of love? (Example: unselfish, devoted).

4. Name ways that we, as individuals, can show our young people that we love them, that they are important to us, and that we want them to have a fulfilling future in the Lord.

5. What can you and I do individually to help the grieving mother of a youth who has committed suicide? Why is it important that we reach out to her? What are some specific ways we can reach out to her?

6. How can we, as concerned Christians, pray for our world's youth and families? What are some positive steps we can take to reduce or eliminate some of the factors (such as availability of weapons, glorification of violence, loneliness, isolation, hopelessness, a sense of worthlessness and/or failure, lack of family stability) that contribute to youth suicide?

HELPING PREVENT YOUTH SUICIDE AS A CONCERNED INDIVIDUAL:

If you notice suicidal behavior in your child, or a friend's child, ask the child if he/she is thinking about suicide. Be direct. Sometimes we think that if we don't talk about suicide, it will go away. It will not. Talk openly. Be willing to listen.

While talking with a youth who may be contemplating suicide, avoid being judgmental and refrain from giving advice. Never dare him or her to do it. Avoid asking why the youth is threatening suicide, since this often encourages defensiveness. Don't be sworn to secrecy but seek support from trusted others: parents, pastor, family physician, school counselor, or psychologist. If a suicide and crisis center is in your area, talk to them about your child. (If the troubled teen is your friend's or church member's child, ask them to contact the center.)

If you suspect a person is thinking about suicide, don't wait. Take immediate action. Your sensitivity and quick response could save a life. Continue to pray for the person, and keep assuring him or her of God's unconditional love.

HELPING PREVENT YOUTH SUICIDE AS A CHURCH OR COMMUNITY:

Organize youth suicide prevention programs and seminars. Some churches have planned church-wide evenings where parents, youth, and church workers can listen to trained Christian counselors talk about suicide prevention.

Contact organizations in your community, local high school counselors, or concerned pastors. Ask them to advise you on how to establish a suicide intervention program in your area.

Provide a safe place where troubled youth can talk to trusted Christian counselors who can help them.

Involve church and community youth in meaningful programs and social activities. In churches, provide youth with weekly programs of Bible study, active leadership roles in church and choir, and regular fun and meaningful activities. Show them they belong to a church that prays for them, a community who loves them, supports them, and cares about the pressures they face.

Prayer: To close your personal devotional time, or your group discussion time, you may want to use the following prayer:

"Our heavenly Father, show us how to reach out with love to women who have had to deal with a child's suicide. Please allow us to love them and to talk with them about their child's death. Help us to be women with open arms and loving hearts. Help our church to be especially sensitive and compassionate with those who are hurting by the loss of a loved one. May we pull close together in troubled times. May we cry together and embrace one another in times of tragedy and confusion. When hearts have been hurt by grief and despair, please show us how to reach out to them. We ask that you would bring healing to their wounded hearts through our loving hearts and caring hands. In Jesus' name, the one who gave the ultimate and eternal gift of love, we pray. Amen."

THOUGHTS, REFLECTIONS AND PRAYERS:

_____
_____
_____
_____
_____
_____
_____
_____
_____
_____
_____
_____
_____
_____
_____
_____
_____
_____
_____
_____
_____
_____
_____
_____
_____
_____
_____
_____
_____
_____
_____

CHAPTER 8: REACHING OUT WITH FAITHFULNESS

Helping Women Cope with Loss and Grief

Bible Study on John 20:1-18

1. Name, read about, and ponder stories told in the Bible of people who stopped and asked faith-searching questions, such as Job, David, Solomon, Jeremiah, Hosea, John the Baptist, and others. What did God reveal to them?

2. Webster's Dictionary describes faithfulness as: "steadfast in affection and allegiance." From your Christian perspective, what could you add to this definition?

3. Mary Magdalene is mentioned fourteen times in the Scriptures. What does this say about her devotion, her faithfulness, her purpose. Read John 19:25. What does this verse tell you about her devotion to Jesus?

4. Name some ways you and I can reach out to a bereaved mother on a deceased child's birthday, anniversary of the death, holidays, and other painful times.

5. Name some physical reactions women might experience after the loss of a child, spouse, or loved one. (For example: gaining or losing weight, not sleeping or sleeping too much, becoming ill, etc.)

6. Name the emotional reactions women might experience after the loss of a loved one. (For example: depression, anger, frustration, etc.)

7. What spiritual reactions might women experience after a loved one's loss? (For example: questioning God's love and faithfulness, questioning God's power, questioning their own faith in God, etc.)

8. Investigate support groups in your church, community, and local area for those dealing with devastating losses. If needed, consider starting a grief support group in your church.

Prayer: To close your personal devotional time, or your group discussion time, you may want to use the following prayer:

"O Lord, so often we don't understand why evil stalks our lives. We don't understand why our children become addicted to drugs, join violent gangs, or die senseless deaths. We are a world of people who are hurt by this evil, who cry in the still hours of the night, who ask the difficult questions of life and faith.

"Be near us when we hurt. Carry us when we can no longer walk in such pain. Deliver us from our suffering and from those who would torment us. Let us look to you for healing and wholeness. Let us learn to depend on your mighty love and faithfulness. Help us to reach out with love and loyalty to those around us who, at this moment, struggle, hurt, and are desperate to be freed from their pain. Help these women to find a new identity, a new hope, and a new purpose in you. Let us be your heart, Lord. And let us be your hands here on Earth. Let us reach out as spiritual sisters to our wounded sisters everywhere. Let us love others as you would have us love. In Jesus' name, we pray. Amen."

THOUGHTS, REFLECTIONS AND PRAYERS:

_____
_____
_____
_____
_____
_____
_____
_____
_____
_____
_____
_____
_____
_____
_____
_____
_____
_____
_____
_____
_____
_____
_____
_____
_____
_____
_____
_____
_____

ABOUT THE AUTHOR

Denise speaks around the world to women's groups, churches, colleges, and seminaries. She teaches "The Writing Minister: How to Write to Publish" to seminarians and pastors at Beeson Divinity School, Samford University, Birmingham, AL. She is married to Dr Timothy George, founding dean of Beeson Divinity School. They are parents of two grown and wonderful children: Christian Timothy George, and Alyce Elizabeth George; and one delightful daughter-in-law (Christian's wife) Rebecca Pounds George.

Denise George is author of more than two dozen books, including: *While the World Watched* (Tyndale House Publishers, 2011, by Carolyn McKinstry with Denise George); *Fighting Fear with Faith* (Christian Focus, 2011); *Johnny Cornflakes: A Story About Loving the Unloved* (Christian Focus, 2010); *The Secret Holocaust Diaries: The Untold Story of Nonna Bannister* (Tyndale House Publishers, 2009); *What Pastors Wish Church Members Knew* (Zondervan, 2009); *What Women Wish Pastors Knew* (Zondervan, 2008).

Other titles from Christian Focus: *God's Gentle Whisper: Developing a Responsive Heart to God* (2007); *Our Dear Child: Letters to your baby on the way* (co-written with her husband, Timothy George, 2006) and *Teach Your Children to Pray* (2004).

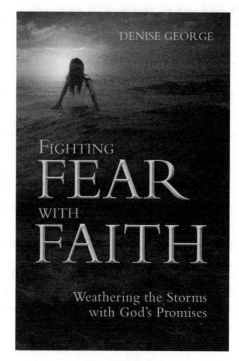

DENISE GEORGE

FIGHTING
FEAR
WITH
FAITH

Weathering the Storms
with God's Promises

ISBN 978-1-84550-716-9

Fighting Fear with Faith

Weathering the Storms with God's Promises

DENISE GEORGE

For many women in difficult situations, fear takes a powerful hold. The reasons, whether real or imagined, abound: the possibility of illness or death; loss or rejection; crime, war or terror; failure or the uncertainty of the future. Some fears are healthy—gifts from God to protect us. Many fears, though, are pretenders—tools of the enemy to harm us.

Fighting Fear with Faith reminds readers of God's great promises and guides us in appropriating God's power. Through stories of people from the Bible and from Christian history, readers will be inspired by portraits of courage and strength. With a complete Bible study guide included, *Fighting Fear with Faith* is ideal for individual or group study.

Like a mighty elm tree that survives a stormy blast, your life—connected to the strong root of Jesus—can withstand the storms.

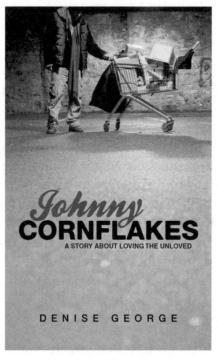

Johnny
CORNFLAKES
A STORY ABOUT LOVING THE UNLOVED

D E N I S E   G E O R G E

ISBN 978-1-84550-551-6

Johnny Cornflakes

A Story about Loving the Unloved

DENISE GEORGE

The heart-warming tale of Johnny Cornflakes is based on a true story, presented in vivid detail by master storyteller Denise George. The narrative offers hope even in difficult places, challenges our attitudes toward others, and shows how God can work in the most unexpected ways through the most unlikely, unloved people.

A tale of pathos and need, of joy and pain, of poverty and glorious abundance.

Dr Calvin Miller

author, poet, artist

The deep things in this simple story tug hard at the heart.

J. I. Packer

Board of Governors' Professor of Theology, Regent College, Vancouver, Canada

Christian Focus Publications
publishes books for all ages

Our mission statement –

STAYING FAITHFUL
In dependence upon God we seek to impact the world through literature faithful to His infallible Word, the Bible. Our aim is to ensure that the Lord Jesus Christ is presented as the only hope to obtain forgiveness of sin, live a useful life and look forward to heaven with Him.

REACHING OUT
Christ's last command requires us to reach out to our world with His gospel. We seek to help fulfil that by publishing books that point people towards Jesus and help them develop a Christ-like maturity. We aim to equip all levels of readers for life, work, ministry and mission.

Books in our adult range are published in three imprints:

Christian Focus contains popular works including biographies, commentaries, basic doctrine and Christian living. Our children's books are also published in this imprint.

Mentor focuses on books written at a level suitable for Bible College and seminary students, pastors, and other serious readers. The imprint includes commentaries, doctrinal studies, examination of current issues and church history.

Christian Heritage contains classic writings from the past.

Christian Focus Publications Ltd,
Geanies House, Fearn, Ross-shire,
IV20 1TW, Scotland, United Kingdom
www.christianfocus.com